Into The Valley Of Death

Craig Wallace

Copyright © 2012 Craig Wallace

All rights reserved.

ISBN: 1480105945
ISBN-13: 978-1480105942

DEDICATION

There are four people in my life who mean the world to me, and without whom I can't imagine what life would be like. This book is dedicated to them.

My daughters, Emily and Erin. Girls, you have both grown into beautiful, young women and I am so proud of you! I know that you will be great successes in life and my proudest accomplishment is being your dad and watching you grow up. I love you both very much.

My two best friends in the world, Carol Anne McEneny, and Jeanne Albert-Cheng, both of Hamilton, Ontario. We rarely talk about love and friendship together, but I can say with no hesitation at all, that I love Carol Anne and Jeanne and with all my heart.

Carol Anne came into my life in November, 2006 when I walked into the store she was working in. Since then my life has changed for the better. Carol Anne, you are my image consultant (I could never now buy clothes without you with me!), my "partner in crime," and, most of all, I am proud to say you are my friend. I love you very much.

I met Jeanne in the summer of 1985 while we both worked at Christie Cookies in Toronto. Since then we have developed a wonderful friendship. Jeanne, you are my friend, my mentor, my confidant, and now my professional colleague. You have a love and passion for life that is contagious, and you always keep me grounded. Jeanne, whatever you do, don't change. I love you, and I need you the way you are!

CONTENTS

Dedication iii
Contents v
Acknowledgements vii
Introduction ix
Into the Valley of Death 5
Chapter I   George Armstrong Custer 7
Chapter II   The Western Frontier 11
Chapter III   Blood on the Plains 21
Chapter IV   An Uneasy Peace 33
Chapter V   The March to War 41
Chapter VI   Blood is Drawn 59
Chapter VII   To the Valley of Death 73
Chapter VIII   Into the Valley of Death 81
Afterword 121
About the Author 129

ACKNOWLEDGEMENTS

There are a number of people I need to thank, as without them this book would never have seen the "light of day."

First, thank you to Jennifer Gault, the owner of Moment 4 Life Photography in Hamilton, Ontario. Jennifer is responsible for the front, back and side covers for "Into the Valley of Death." (She was assisted with the front cover by Hamilton based artist, Heidi Dakin.) Jennifer is a brilliant photographer and I highly recommend her for any photographic needs that you may have. She can be reached at Moment4lifephotography@live.ca and at 1-905-730-8613.

Thank you to Howard Rosenthal of Sarasota, Florida for his editing assistance with the manuscript.

Thank you to Nick Cheng of Dundas, Ontario for his invaluable work in formatting and uploading the draft.

INTRODUCTION

Many books about the Battle of Little Big Horn in 1876 have been written in the last 136 years. There have been traditional historical analyses, scholarly works, fictional accounts, etc. What I have tried to do with "Into the Valley of Death" is something different. I have combined the approach of explaining the history of the event in a formal or even at times scholarly fashion, along with a historical fictional account of the events of the actual battle. My goal when I wrote this was to educate and to entertain.

The challenges of writing about this battle are many. None of the soldiers who fought with Lieutenant Colonel George Armstrong Custer's five companies of soldiers survived that day. The Native American victors were reluctant in many cases to describe what they had seen in the battle for fear of retribution from white society. So we are left with fragments of information to work with. Some native accounts of the battle, and, what we could ascertain from the carnage of the battlefield, is how the events of that day in 1876 have come to be understood and written about.

Dialogue amongst the soldiers before, during, and after the battle scenes is of course, fictionalized. However even with that, I have striven to ensure that the historical context of when and where those conversations were depicted, are accurate to the very best of my ability.

I hope you enjoy reading this book as much as I have enjoyed writing it.

Craig Wallace
Hamilton, Ontario
September 2012

INTO THE VALLEY OF DEATH

Sunday June 25, 1876 – Late Afternoon
Montana Territory

Lieutenant Colonel George Armstrong Custer, his Remington sporting rifle clenched tightly in his hands, glanced over the top of the barricade of dead horses and he peered through the clouds of gun smoke and dust hovering over the top of the hill that he and his soldiers were dug into. There was a brief lull in the fighting. All around him he could hear screams and moans of wounded soldiers along with bellows from the dying horses. From every direction around him he could hear war whoops and battle cries from the seemingly thousands of enraged Lakota[1] and Cheyenne warriors that had his small, decimated force of cavalrymen surrounded on the hill-top. Custer, like all the remaining United States cavalrymen, was filthy, caked in dirt and black gunpowder grime. He had blood splatters on his shirt and buckskin pants as a result of blood spraying from nearby wounded and dead soldiers.

"My god" he thought. "I fight through and survive Bull Run, Gettysburg, Appomattox, and Washita with hardly even a scratch. Does it really end here, on this god forsaken hill in the middle of

---

[1] Commonly known as Sioux by the Whites, the Lakota were the Sioux who lived in the westernmost portion of the Great Plains and Prairie region of Canada.

nowhere?"

His thoughts were interrupted by his adjutant, Lieutenant William Cooke. Cooke was known by the troopers as "The Queen's Own" due to the fact that he had been born and raised in Hamilton, Ontario before traveling to Buffalo, New York, to attend school and later enlist in the United States Army. He had served Custer loyally since 1866. Cooke crawled over to Custer, staying low to avoid attracting Indian fire.

"General" Cooke began. "There isn't much time left. The hostiles will be back and we don't have a lot to try and hold them off with. I count less than 30 unwounded men left. We have another 15 or so walking wounded who can fight. The men's Springfields are jamming up as you had predicted they would, and because of that we can't get sustained volley firing going. Even without the jamming problem, we don't have enough ammunition or men to last much longer. I see no sign that Benteen is coming. Sir, I really don't think we are going to get out of this."

Custer looked sadly at him. "Thanks Cookie. I think you are right. We did give it a good try, didn't we?"

Lieutenant Cooke stared back at the officer he had served so proudly for over 10 years now. "Yes sir, we did" he answered, and gave Custer a sharp salute.

Captain Tom Custer, the younger brother of "General" Custer,[2] interrupted the moment. Captain Custer, yelled; "The red devils are coming again men. Let's send them to hell where they belong!"

---

[2] In this age the US Army used a system of "Brevet" or temporary ranks awarded to officers for bravery and exceptional service in combat. Custer had been promoted to the "Brevet" rank of Major General in the Civil War. After the war his rank was reduced to Captain and eventually he was promoted to Lieutenant Colonel. His official rank at time of death was Lieutenant Colonel but by protocol he and others in his situation were referred to by the highest rank they had achieved.

CHAPTER I
GEORGE ARMSTRONG CUSTER

George Armstrong Custer was born in New Rumley, Ohio, on December 5, 1839. At an early age he moved with his family to Monroe, Michigan. From his early boyhood days, "Autie" (as he was affectionately known as by his family) had a strong interest in all things military. Family members recalled young Autie walking around the house declaring, "My voice is for war!"

After a truly undistinguished public school stint he entered the United States Military Academy at West Point, New York. There he continued his record of being a poor student. Custer was not interested in academics and he grew restless under the strict, almost stifling discipline of West Point. On several occasions he came close to flunking out entirely but was always able to save himself just before crossing that line.

In the spring of 1861, the United States was embroiled in turmoil as the southern states began leaving the Union to form the Confederate States of America. Many young cadets from those southern states at West Point, including close classmates of Custer, were emotionally torn. Do they honor the oath they swore to the United States when they entered West Point, or do they honor their homes and return to the South? For Custer and those who stayed, action came soon.

Right after graduation Custer, and his fellow graduates, were thrown into combat as the Civil War engulfed the United States. It was during the Civil War that Custer proved that being a good soldier on the battlefield was far more important than being a good soldier in the classroom. He was a natural born soldier/cavalryman.

Custer believed in leading his troops from the front, and his favorite tactic was a front-on charge into the enemy with himself at the head of his men. On numerous occasions Custer's commands defeated numerically superior Confederate forces. Credit for these victories was usually given Custer's almost "incredible" aggressiveness. Custer never showed fear or restraint in battle. His only goal was the utter defeat of his enemy. Nowhere was he more at home than in the pursuit of an enemy. In this situation, Custer was like a wolf tracking wounded prey. He would never, ever, let up until his "prey" had been found and destroyed.

Many fellow officers accused Custer of being overly reckless or even careless with the lives of his men during Civil War action. But truth be told, Custer was very careful about planning his attacks. He surveyed the territory precisely, and thoughtfully planned his troop movements. When he sent his forces into action, he was always at the head of his men. Custer, unlike more modern Generals, believed that a leader led from the front and he would not ask his men to do anything that he was not willing to do himself. It was due to this characteristic that Custer gained the almost "blind loyalty" of his troops.

In 1863, in the crucial battle of Gettysburg that some historians have argued changed the course of the war and led to the Union's eventual victory, it was Custer who, leading a small, outnumbered regiment of Union cavalry, smashed a charge by legendary Confederate cavalry General Jeb Stuart. Custer rode at the front of his men and personally led them in their charge against Stuart's forces. His crushing of Stuart turned around the course of this battle and as a result, the entire war.

At age 23 Custer was given a "Brevet" (or temporary) promotion to Brigadier General, making him the youngest ever General in United States history. As his "star rose" even higher in countless battles, he was further promoted to Major General, which was the rank he held at the end of the Civil War.

In the spring of 1865 it was Custer who personally helped bring about the final collapse of the Confederacy. He led his forces in an unending, unmerciful pursuit of the Confederate Army of Northern Virginia, commanded by the legendary General Robert E. Lee. Lee, one the greatest, American born Generals ever, simply could not "shake" Custer's forces. Lee finally surrendered to the United States forces led by General Ulysses S Grant at Appomattox. Present at the surrender was Major General George Armstrong Custer. With the surrender of Lee, the back of the Confederacy was broken forever, and the Civil War ended shortly afterwards.

At the end of the war, George Custer decided to remain in the Army. He was popular with his superiors and well known in the media of the time. He was called "The Boy General" by the American media. He was slim, had long blonde hair and vivid blue eyes. He fairly "bristled" with nervous energy. Many commented that you could feel the energy radiating in waves off of him. Unless he was asleep, George Armstrong Custer was always on the move. He had excellent manners, although he had a high-pitched voice, and could tend to be "brusque." "Autie" was articulate, well read, and was considered quite "dashing" by the ladies. (Regardless of what the ladies of the time thought however, Custer had married a beautiful young lady by the name of Elizabeth (Libbie) Bacon in 1863 and was utterly devoted to her.)

CHAPTER II
THE WESTERN FRONTIER

In 1866, Custer was promoted in rank to that of Lieutenant Colonel and given command of the brand new 7th Cavalry Regiment. The 7th Cavalry was posted on the western frontier, and Custer was well aware that he would now face the challenge of subduing hostile Indians and protecting white settlers. He looked forward to testing his military command and combat skills against a new foe.

His first test against the Indians came the following year in what became known as "Hancock's' War." It was a disaster for him. Custer and the 7th Cavalry spent the summer of 1867 futilely chasing Sioux and Cheyenne warriors across the Great Plains. On more than one occasion Custer exclaimed to his officers "Why won't the Indians stand and fight?" He found their tactics to be very frustrating – even enraging.

The reason why Indians would not stand and fight his troops was very simple – they didn't want to die! The army's greatest advantage over the Indians was firepower and discipline. The Indians had no intention whatsoever of allowing the soldiers to use that advantage. They would use "hit and run attacks" on army columns. At dawn they would quickly attack the sentries that were guarding the army's horses and then disappear when more soldiers came to the aid of the sentries. Or they would strike quickly at the advance guard of a column before disappearing. They would only stand and fight soldiers if they had an overwhelming advantage in manpower or if they were defending their village from attack. In the latter case, they would break off hostilities as soon as the women and children of the village were safe. Custer was expecting them to fight like his Confederate enemies of the Civil War, and that simply wasn't going to happen.

Towards the end of the frustrating summer of 1867, Custer was alerted to a cholera outbreak back east. He left his command to check on the welfare of his wife Elizabeth, who was staying at Fort Hays, Kansas, where the 7th had been stationed. For that shocking lapse in judgment, Custer was court-martialed, found guilty of Dereliction of Duty, and suspended from active duty for a year. Considering Custer had been known for ordering the summary execution of captured deserters, his decision to abandon his command to check on his wife was deplorable and hypocritical to say the least.

The suspension didn't last for a year, however. General Philip Sheridan reinstated Custer to active duty in the fall of 1868. The United States government had decided that the Cheyenne nation needed to be punished for various alleged atrocities against white settlers across the Great Plains. To punish them, they needed a soldier who would pursue them to the gates of Hell if that were what was needed. Sheridan, who Custer had served under during the Civil War, could think of nobody better suited for that job then George Armstrong Custer.

Upon receiving Sheridan's telegram ordering him back to active duty, Custer hurried westwards from Monroe, Michigan, to Fort Hays. Custer had his regiment on the move shortly after reaching the fort.

Before he did that he made two significant changes to the regiment.

Always conscious of appearance (he was known in the Civil War to wear very flamboyant hand made uniforms) Custer decided to arrange the companies of the 7th Cavalry by color of horse. All the "Bay" colored horses would be in one company, all the "Sorrels" in another, etc. This move upset many soldiers and officers who were familiar with their mounts, their personalities, and "quirks." Now they may possibly have to get familiar with a new horse just as they were leaving on a major campaign. There were numerous protests over this policy of Custer's but he stood firm. And the 7th would now be the sharpest looking outfit in the West!

The second change occurred when he watched his troopers during drills and became quite concerned over their lack of accurate marksmanship. He ordered increased marksmanship training, and in addition ordered Lieutenant William Cooke to create an elite force of 40 sharpshooters. This force, led by Cooke, would be the 7th's elite "shock-troops."

Custer also decided to bring the regimental band along on the campaign. Again, to add to the "flash and style" of the 7th he had created the band and decided that the "theme" or "marching" song of the 7th would be an old Irish drinking song by the name of "Garry Owen."

It was cold marching west across the Great Plains that fall. But Custer seemed impervious to the cold and drove his men and the horses unmercifully hard. He had developed a reputation during the Civil War of being almost immune from fatigue and he showed on this campaign that he had not changed. The soldiers were marching 12 hours or more per day and the temperatures kept dropping as winter approached. For two solid days the regiment was engulfed in a major blizzard. The soldiers and horses were caked in snow and ice and many of the troopers came down with frost- bite. But Custer would not stop or even slow down. The 7th Cavalry pushed on through the blinding snow and bitter cold. Custer was in his element here - pursuing an enemy in the same manner, as a wolf would track wounded, bleeding prey.

On a bitterly cold November 26th Custer's main scout, California Joe, reported a large trail in the snow made by Indian ponies leading to the Washita River in what is now modern day Oklahoma. The 7th Cavalry Regiment marched briskly following the trail, and just before nightfall, Custer's scouts reported a large Cheyenne village along the Washita River. Custer grinned – the wolf had found his prey.

Gathering his officer's together, Custer outlined his attack plan. The regiment would be divided into 4 battalions and be positioned so as to surround village.

"I want no noise as this is done," Custer ordered. "There is to be complete silence as we have to catch them by total surprise. If the hostiles catch wind that we are here, the village will break and run. Nothing moves faster on the plains than an Indian village on the run. I don't even want the men to stamp their feet to try and stay warm. At dawn I will order a single rifle to be fired and the band will begin "Garry Owen." That will be the signal to attack. Kill all the warriors and anyone else who resists. Try and take the women and children prisoner, but don't take casualties just to take prisoners. Any questions?"

There were some more brief discussions among the officers and then the regiment split into the ordained 4 battalions. Once each battalion was in position the soldiers waited. It was a long, brutally cold night. Due to the need for total surprise the soldiers could not light fires, or even move around to try and stay warm. The only way of trying to gain some warmth came from sips of whiskey from the many flasks hidden among the soldiers.

At dawn a single rifle shot echoed across the Great Plains, and the band started into "Garry Owen." (Due to the sub-zero temperatures the band didn't progress very far as the brass instruments quickly froze up.) The 7th went into action. Cavalry bugles blared out charge! Soldiers unlimbered their rifles and pistols and charged into the village. As was the case in the Civil War, Custer was at the head of his men, leading the charge. Sleepy warriors sprang out their bedrolls and charged from their teepees only to be cut down by soldier's gunfire. Many soldiers formed into pairs and held a rope between them. They charged the teepees with one soldier charging to the left and the other to the right of a teepee with the rope between them. The rope would hit the teepee and knock it over leaving the occupants exposed to the soldier's gunfire.

This wasn't a battle – it was a slaughter. The warriors tried to form some form of defense, but most were cut down before many could even fire a single arrow or gun shot. Despite Custer's orders to save women and children many of them were killed in the chaos of battle. A number of female Cheyenne desperately fought back alongside the warriors in an effort to hold the soldiers off long enough to save their children. Because they took up arms, and joined in the fighting, the soldiers showed them no mercy, they were brutally killed alongside the male warriors.

Despite the best efforts of the soldiers, many Indians did manage to escape. Major Joel H Elliott, one of Custer's favorite officers, spotted a large group of women and children who had broken out of the village and were escaping. Elliott took 19 soldiers and took off in hot pursuit yelling as he did so "Here goes, for a Brevet or a coffin."

As Major Elliott galloped off with his small force, the remaining soldiers began "mopping up." Custer was pleased with what he saw – the Cheyenne had been totally defeated. Knowing however that many had escaped, Custer wanted to ensure that nothing would be left for them.

"Burn the teepees," he ordered. "Lieutenant Cooke, take your sharpshooters and go to the hostiles' pony herd and shoot all the ponies. I want nothing left here that any hostile can use against us."

Cooke gathered up his force of sharp shooters and rode to where the Cheyenne had their pony herd. The soldiers then methodically began shooting each animal. As the guns began firing, the captured women and children began wailing inconsolably. As their lodges and teepees began going up in flames, along with their warm clothes and food that had been gathered for the winter, the volume of hysterics grew louder. Custer ignored them. This was harsh – he admitted that. However, by killing the horses and destroying their homes and supplies, he knew he had shattered this village's ability to wage war against white settlers.

As Custer was supervising the destruction of the village, his younger brother Lieutenant Tom Custer rode up. Tom, like his older brother, had been assigned to the 7th Cavalry in 1866. But while George was always willing to help his younger brother's career, Tom had already proven that he was in his own right a superb soldier. During the Civil War, he became the first American soldier in history to win two Congressional Medals of Honor-the highest award an American soldier can win. Tom, like his famous older brother was a dashing and very brave soldier. George Custer used his influence to get Tom assigned to the 7th however, Tom's rise in the army was clearly on his own merit.

"Autie", (as the Custer family referred to George) Tom said as he rode up. "The red bastards got me. Look at this." He showed his brother a bloody arm wound he had just received.

George quickly looked at him. 'I'll think you'll be fine, but have the surgeon look at it just to be sure. It's nothing like you received previously", he added with a smile, referring to Tom's horrific facial wound received during the Civil War while earning one of his Medals of Honor.

INTO THE VALLEY OF DEATH

Lieutenant Edward Godfrey then galloped up.

"General, oh, and you too Lieutenant" he began, nodding at Tom Custer. "There is a large group of hostiles approaching us very fast. Some of the Indians must have escaped the village here and spread the word that we have attacked. There must be more villages that we can't see from here, and the warriors are coming from there."

Custer peered through his binoculars and saw a huge force of hostile warriors riding hard towards his regiment. Knowing right away that they heavily outnumbered him, he gave the order for the 7th Cavalry to withdraw. Upon hearing that order, Captain Frederick Benteen rode to Custer's side.

"General, Major Elliott has not returned yet. We can't leave without him," Benteen implored.

"Captain Benteen, there is a large force of hostiles approaching us. They outnumber us and I have to think of the overall well being of the entire regiment. We can't fight them and keep control of the prisoners. I am sure Major Elliott is and will be okay and will catch up with us. We are pulling out now."

"So we are abandoning Major Elliott? Is that right, General?" Benteen asked with cold fury in his eyes.

Custer, who had a very uneasy relationship with Benteen, stared right back at him. "Carry out your orders, Captain" he said, with an edge in his voice.

Tom Custer added "Captain, with all due respect the General here has made his decision. It is our duty to carry out his orders. I intend to do so. I suggest that it would be prudent for you to do that as well."

Without another word, Benteen turned his horse around and rode away. Saying he disliked Custer would be charitable. He hated Custer personally and had little or no respect for Custer as a professional military officer. However, Frederick Benteen was an outstanding officer himself (Custer disliked Benteen immensely, however he did respect his professional abilities), and he wasn't one to disobey orders. Custer had given the order to withdraw and Benteen would carry those orders out.

The 7th Cavalry pulled out of the immense burning village with the captured women and children. Custer, in order to ensure the hostiles would not attack him, first made a feint towards the approaching warriors and the villages from which they had come. The warriors pulled back in order to protect their homes. When night came, Custer then ordered the 7th to swing 180 degrees and begin a withdrawal back towards Fort Hays.

Once Custer and the 7th Cavalry had successfully executed their withdrawal, warriors from the neighboring villages entered the shattered Cheyenne village alongside the Washita River. The village was burned to the ground and dead bodies were scattered everywhere. The warriors were stunned beyond words when they came across the massacred pony herd. Never had they witnessed such cold-blooded slaughter as they saw here. They simply could not believe that fellow humans would, and without any apparent misgivings, shoot helpless animals. From that day forward, Custer would be known to the Plains Indians as "Creeping Panther" or "Son of the Morning Star." Both names were in regard to his tactic of silently approaching a village and attacking at dawn.

The 7th Cavalry returned to Fort Hays with great fanfare. This was a huge victory for both the army and Custer personally. The army had suffered a major defeat at the hands of the Sioux Indians in December 1866 when Captain William J Fetterman and his entire command of 81 men were wiped out in a short savage battle. Custer and the army had chased the Indians all across the Great Plains through the summer of 1867 with no success. Now they could boast of victory. Custer had proven he could not only fight and defeat Confederates, he could also defeat Indians.

The only negative was the fate of Major Elliott and his small force. He did not rejoin the regiment after their withdrawal from the village and there had been no sign of him since. In mid December the army sent an expedition back to the site of the destroyed village. There they found what remained of Major Elliott and his men. It was clear what had happened. Major Elliott's command had run right into the large force of hostiles that Custer retreated from. Elliott had ordered his men to dismount from their horses, lie down and form a circle with their feet pointing inwards. They fought in that manner until their ammunition was exhausted and they were overrun. The Cheyenne warriors killed Elliott and his men and then stripped and mutilated their bodies.

When this discovery was made, and the news was spread, back at the fort Captain Benteen openly criticized Custer for what he called his "abandonment of Major Elliott." Some members of the 7th agreed with Benteen, while others while very upset at the death of the popular officer felt Custer had done the right thing and could not have saved Elliott. As many of the 7th said, "if Custer had attempted to find Major Elliott –who had recklessly galloped off on his own initiative, – all he would have accomplished is to turn the great victory at Washita into a bloody defeat."

The following year, Custer bolstered his image as a great Indian fighter by pursuing the largest group of Cheyenne on the Great Plains until the Cheyenne finally grew weary of Custer's unrelenting pursuit and agreed to meet with United States Government officials and sign a peace treaty. Part of the treaty required the Cheyenne to give up their nomadic ways and live on reservations. The Cheyenne, like Robert E Lee and other Confederates in the Civil War, simply found they could not "shake" the "Boy General" once he had found their trail.

But George Armstrong Custer wasn't the only army officer battling Indians, nor were the Cheyenne the only nemesis of the US Army.

CHAPTER III
BLOOD ON THE PLAINS

Before and after Custer initially engaged hostiles on the Plains for the first time, other Army units felt the wrath of Native Americans. The Army's main nemesis was the Lakota.

The Lakota (Sioux) Nation was the largest Plains Indian tribe in North America. Since the late 1850's there had been repeated clashes between the U.S. Army and Sioux warriors across the Great Plains. In 1862, during the height of the Civil War, the Santee Sioux [3] went on a bloody rampage. The Santee had signed a treaty with the U.S. Government agreeing to live on a reservation in Minnesota in return for food, housing, education, etc. As a result of government corruption, food was not getting to the reservation and the Sioux were starving. When they complained, the government official responsible for that reservation sneeringly said; "if they are hungry let them eat grass." (It is important to note here, that while the Federal Government in Washington rightly gets blamed for many "screw

---

[3] The Sioux were not one homogeneous group. They were divided up into the various "factions" such as the San Arc, Hunk Papa, Oglala, Brule, Minneconjou, Two Kettles, and Blackfeet (who were mainly in Western Canada).

ups" they could not be blamed for this. Congress had properly set aside funds for food for the Sioux and the food had been purchased with those funds. It was the local government agent who diverted the food away from the Sioux to the black market who was to blame.)

When Chief Little Crow who had been attempting to keep peace among his warriors and government officials, heard that, he ceased in his efforts to restrain his warriors. Warriors murdered the reservation agent and his body found with his mouth stuffed with grass. The Santee then launched attacks across Minnesota. Entire towns and farms were burned to the ground and hundreds of innocent whites slaughtered. General John Pope was ordered to take an entire army away from Civil War action and rush to Minnesota to subdue the Santee. The fighting between Pope's troops and the Santee was ferocious. However, due to superior firepower and military planning and discipline, the U.S. Army emerged victorious. In December 1862 the largest mass execution in American history took place at a Federal penitentiary in Mankato, Minnesota. By the direct order of President Abraham Lincoln, 36 Santee warriors, including Little Crow, were hung in revenge for their atrocities.

In 1864 in an area of modern day Colorado known as Sand Creek, Colonel John Chivington led a force of soldiers in an attack on a Cheyenne (the Sioux and Cheyenne were traditional allies) village. Cheyenne warriors had been guilty of several unprovoked attacks on white settlements in the area, and Chivington was determined to punish them. Before the attack, Chivington had ordered his men to kill all the Indians they encountered. When one officer expressed concern over the killing of children Chivington responded "Kill them all. Nits make lice."

Chivington's men did their very best to follow his orders. They attacked at dawn and slaughtered the Indians as they emerged from their teepees. Few escaped the soldiers' wrath. When the "battle" was over, Chivington and his men scalped and further mutilated the bodies of the dead Indians. After burning the village to the ground, Chivington's troops withdrew and returned to Denver. There they paraded victoriously through the streets of Denver with Indian scalps, breasts and genitals hanging from their hats and saddles and numerous Indian heads on poles.

Many whites decried the barbarism (in particular the mutilations) exhibited by Colonel Chivington and his troops. However, the soldiers defended their actions by claiming they were simply seeking revenge for similar atrocities carried out by the Santee Sioux in Minnesota two years earlier.

The Cheyenne and their Sioux allies vowed revenge, and they got it in December 1866 in an isolated area of modern-day Wyoming close to an army outpost known as Fort Phil Kearny. The army had built a series of forts across the Great Plains along what was known as "The Bozeman Trail." This trail had been "blazed across" the Plains by explorer John Bozeman, and was used by settlers as they headed west towards in most cases, California. The forts were built to ensure a strong military presence along the trail. The "flashpoint" of the entire trail, indeed the entire Great Plains, became Fort Phil Kearny.

Colonel Henry Carrington had been assigned the duty of building and then commanding Fort Phil Kearny. He decided on building the fort in an area that offered the best protection for the garrison. He wanted to ensure there were no trees or hills directly around the stockade walls so sentries could clearly see anyone approaching the walls. The downside was the closest wood that could be used for construction was several miles away. Everyday parties of woodcutters would leave the site of the fort to cut wood for use in constructing the fort's buildings. And everyday Sioux warriors would attack or otherwise harass the woodcutters. This constant harassment of the wood cutting parties necessitated the use of military escorts for those parties.

Colonel Carrington was a cautious officer and he constantly worried that the military escorts he sent out would find themselves pursuing the attacking warriors and as a result be ambushed and cut off. As a consequence, all escorts were given strict orders to simply drive the warriors away – never pursue them. This rankled many of the soldiers – especially two Civil War veterans Captains William J Fetterman and Frederick Brown. Neither Fetterman (who was a well respected combat officer) nor Brown had any respect for Indians. They felt Carrington was being cautious – they truly felt he was a coward and they "itched" for a chance to whip the Indians. Fetterman had boasted in early December 1866: "Give me 80 good men and I'll ride through the whole Sioux nation."

On December 21, 1866, Fetterman got his chance. It was a bitterly cold morning when the word cutting party set out with a small group of soldiers escorting it. As they approached the wooded area, Sioux warriors appeared. They were led by a man whose name would become legendary (or in some eyes infamous) across North America and still to this day is seen as one of the greatest fighting leaders in North American history. The man was Crazy Horse.

Crazy Horse was not a "leader" in the traditional military sense, as a soldier would understand. Indian warriors fought as individuals and followed leaders who they felt were brave and capable. Indian chiefs and leaders could not compel others to obey or follow them. They led by example. Crazy Horse had already proven his bravery and fighting abilities in earlier clashes with soldiers and in numerous battles with rival tribes such as the Crow Indians. On December 6th, he had led a group of warriors against the wood-cutting party and had nearly managed to convince Captain Fetterman, who had commanded a relief column of troops, to follow his warriors into an ambush. Fetterman only held up due to the tight restrictions Carrington had placed on him. On December 21st, Crazy Horse was going to try again.

As the small military force escorting the woodcutters began firing at the approaching warriors, Colonel Carrington organized a relief column. It was a chaotic scene as soldiers ran for their horses with the sounds of gun fire and Indian battle cries in the air. Fetterman, who wanted his chance to whip the Sioux Nation, ran up to Carrington and said; "Sir, I am the most senior officer next to you and I respectively demand the honor of commanding the relief column."

Carrington hesitated. Fetterman was correct in that he should be given command. On the other hand he didn't trust him to follow his orders. He decided to allow Fetterman to command the column but to "keep him on a tight leash."

"Captain, command of the column is yours. But listen closely. Pull in your horns here. You are to relieve the wood cutting party and then return. You are not to pursue the hostiles. In particular you will not pursue them past Lodge Trail Ridge[4]. Do you understand these orders, Captain?"

Fetterman sullenly responded, "Yes sir, I do." He, of course, had no intention of following the orders of an officer who he considered to be a coward.

Captain Brown, a close friend of Fetterman, rode up and asked "Mind if I join you?"

Fetterman was pleased to have his friend with him. "C'mon Fred" he answered. Let's go whip those red bastards."

The relief column consisted of 49 infantry soldiers armed with obsolete, Civil War era, single shot muzzle loading muskets and 27

---

[4] Lodge Trail Ridge is a ridge-line that leads to a series of valleys and gully's a mile or so from the fort.

cavalry soldiers armed with 7 shot Spencer carbines. Lieutenant George Grummond – yet another critic of Carrington who was itching for action, commanded the cavalry. Just before heading through gates of the fort, two civilians James Wheatly and Isaac Fisher rode up. Both were carrying brand new, state of the art, 16-shot Henry repeating rifles. Wheatley called out;

"Captain, can Isaac and I join you? We want to try out our new rifles on the red devils."

Fetterman nodded his approval and the column headed out. The cavalry was in the lead with the infantry trotting along as fast as they could, bringing up the rear.

As the relief column approached, Crazy Horse and his warriors pulled back just out of rifle range. They shouted insults at Fetterman and his men. They taunted them and bent over their horses baring their buttocks at the soldiers. Fetterman, Brown, and Grummond bristled at the insults, and at what they perceived to be Carrington's sheer lack of courage. Fetterman finally had enough. He looked at his fellow officers and said;

"I am not going to sit here and let that coward Carrington turn me and my men into women. We are going to show those bastards what American soldiers can do. Let's get them!"

The soldiers set off in hot pursuit of Crazy Horse with loud battle cries of their own. The warriors raced away over Lodge Trail Ridge with the cavalry in hot pursuit and the infantry bringing up the rear.

The soldiers poured over the ridge and down into a valley. The fleeing warriors stayed just out of rifle range encouraging the soldiers to try and close the gap. Once the infantry came over the ridge and entered the valley, a scene from hell erupted in front of Fetterman's entire force. Hundreds, maybe thousands, of enraged Sioux warriors who had been carefully hiding, sprang from behind rocks, bushes, etc., and began a rain of arrows and bullets down into the trapped soldiers. More Indians sealed off the entrance to the valley from where the soldiers had come through. The soldiers were now trapped. Their only hope was to try to hang on long enough for a relief column from the fort to reach them.

The infantry died first. Armed with only single shot muskets and with no cover to shelter behind, they were quickly wiped out before most had gotten off a handful of shots.

Captain Fetterman, further into the valley, tried to organize a defense but his cavalry troopers were split up and seeking cover wherever they could find it. There was no way to organize a defensive stand as the soldiers were being hit from all sides with arrows, bullets, and even rocks. Lieutenant Grummond and the main bulk of the cavalry were wiped out in one area of the valley after a short but fierce firefight. Fetterman and Brown along with another small group of troopers, took cover behind some rocks and began a desperate fight for survival. Armed with the 7-shot Spencer carbine, the cavalry troopers were able to put up a better fight than did the infantry, but the end result was the same. One by one the troopers fell, and both Fetterman and Brown realized they were doomed. There was a saying on the Great Plains; "Save the last bullet for yourself" as being captured alive by Indians was a horrific fate nobody could imagine.

As warriors began advancing on Fetterman's position, he realized there were only moments left. He turned to Captain Brown, and screamed "Fred get over here."

Captain Brown scrambled over to his friend, revolver in hand. "I'm here Will," he said.

Fetterman fired a shot towards the Indians with his Colt revolver and then looked at his old comrade. "Fred", he said with a husky tone to his voice. "I am so sorry, I was wrong and Carrington was right. And now if we don't act right away those red bastards will get us."

Brown nodded. "It's okay Will, I am ready. We both know what we have to do now."

They both looked at each other in the eyes and placed the muzzle of their revolvers against the other's temple.

Fetterman yelled "One."

Brown added; "Two."

Fetterman answered; "Three."

At the count of three, both officers pulled the triggers and dropped to the ground with their brains blown out.

Close by where Captains Fetterman and Brown died, James Wheatly and Isaac Fisher put up a furious, determined, resistance. These two men were tough Civil War veterans, experienced frontiersmen, and were each armed with a 16-shot Henry repeating rifle - the finest weapon of the day. Joined by a small cluster of troopers, they sheltered behind a rock formation and Wheatley and Fisher in particular pumped a devastating fire into the surrounding Sioux. The two civilians kneeled back to back and picked off warrior after warrior who tried to assault their position. Any Sioux who showed his head quickly had a Henry round crashing through it in short order. The troopers, with their Spencer carbines, drew courage from Wheatley and Fisher, and added to the growing carnage of dead and wounded Indians. Faced with such overwhelming firepower, the Sioux pulled back for a short period of time, giving the soldiers hope that if they could just hold out a while longer perhaps a relief column from Fort Phil Kearny could reach them. They knew Colonel Carrington would send more troops to their aid when he heard the beginning of the firefight.

And indeed Carrington was responding. He was peering through his binoculars when he spotted Fetterman disobey his orders and take his column over Lodge Trail Ridge. Immediately, Carrington felt a sense of dread. He quickly ordered Captain Ten Eyk to organize another relief column and move out. As Captain Ten Eyk was doing so, the fort began hearing heavy firing from past the ridge. It was clear that Fetterman had gotten the battle he so badly and desperately craved. The firing grew more and more intense, and Carrington urged Ten Eyk to get going. Carrington sensed Fetterman and his men were in dreadful, even mortal danger.

With the gunfire still ringing out, the relief column galloped out of the fort's gates heading to the sound of the firing. The question was, could they reach Fetterman and his men in time?

Wheatley, Fisher, despite their best efforts and overwhelming courage, and the cavalry troopers huddled with them couldn't last. With all the remaining soldiers on the battlefield dead, close to a thousand warriors turned their attention to their position. Hundreds of bullets, arrows, and rocks came crashing into the stronghold in a furious rain of death. Casualties among the small group of holdouts began to mount and the rate of fire as a result slowed down. When the soldiers' fire slackened, warriors, enraged at the casualties they had suffered at the hands of the whites here, charged in swinging clubs and finished off the wounded. The final soldier standing was Trumpeter Adolph Metzger, an immigrant from Germany. Metzger had fought bravely, using his Spencer carbine to deadly effect against the Sioux. With Wheatley and Fisher down, his other comrades dead, and his Spencer out of ammunition, Metzger stared in horror as Sioux warriors swarmed in. Not prepared to go quietly he grabbed his bugle and began swinging it at enemy heads while loudly cursing them in German. He was finally dispatched with a war club blow to his head.

The battlefield now grew quiet. The warriors, in revenge for the Sand

Creek massacre, attacked the soldiers' bodies with a bloody vengeance. Heads were pounded flat with stone war clubs. Bodies were cut open and entrails pulled out. Eyes were gouged out and genitals chopped off.

Just as the mutilations were completed, Captain Ten Eyk and the relief column came onto the scene. It had arrived too late. As the soldiers approached the battlefield, the warriors pulled back. A scene of unimaginable horror greeted the American soldiers. Their comrades had been chopped up and mutilated in the most horrific, grotesque manner.

They could see isolated areas where soldiers had attempted to make a stand. The infantry were grouped together in death. Lieutenant Grummond's body was found with a large cluster of dead cavalrymen and horses. They found Fetterman and Brown together with bullet holes in their temples and powder burns on the skin surrounding the wounds, indicating suicide.

When they came to the Wheatley-Fisher position, they found both civilians surrounded by a "mountain" of spent Henry cartridges, showing they had unleashed a devastating barrage of gunfire at the Indians. All around the position were blood trails and huge blood splatters (the Indians had carried off their own dead and wounded) showing that Wheatley and Fisher along with the soldiers with them had sold their own lives very dearly. The one body left un-mutilated was that of Adolph Metzger. His body was found relatively intact covered by a blanket of all things, with his battered and dented bugle beside him. Years later, Sioux warriors who had taken part in the battle spoke of the tremendous courage shown by the German bugler and they showed their respect in return by leaving him intact. (In contrast the same warriors expressed great respect for the courage of James Wheatley and Isaac Fisher however they wreaked a terrible vengeance upon their bodies – apparently in fury over how many warriors these two men had killed.)

Americans were stunned by the news of the "Fetterman Massacre" as it became known as. Captain William Fetterman, while not a national hero in any sense had been a very distinguished Civil War officer. The idea that such an experienced combat officer could lead a group of trained soldiers armed with modern weapons, into total disaster against "savages" not quite out of the Stone Age was simply unbelievable to most Americans.

1867 was a bloody year across the Great Plains. Hancock's War raged most of the summer. Soldiers and Sioux warriors clashed at the "Wagon Box Fight" and the "Hayfield Fight." Numerous white settlements were attacked and destroyed as the army tried unsuccessfully to protect them. Political pressure mounted on Washington to get the Indian problem solved and make the western frontier open and safe for settlement by whites.

In the spring of 1868, US Government officials and army officers met with Oglala Chief Red Cloud and other Sioux Warriors, and over a period of weeks negotiated what would become known as the 1868 Treaty of Fort Laramie. The terms brought peace to the west, but were very controversial. In the minds of many whites, the treaty was too easy on the Indians and the United States had given up far too much.

For one, this treaty marked the very first (and to date only) time the United States signed a treaty ending a war by giving up land. The United States agreed as part of the treaty to abandon all the forts built along the Bozeman Trail. This included Fort Phil Kearny for which the army had paid such a high price to defend.

Second, the United States acknowledged that the Paha Sapa (Black Hills) of modern day South Dakota was sovereign Sioux land forever. This was a "deal breaker" for Red Cloud and the Sioux, as the Black Hills were the most holy of all places in their religion and culture. It was believed that Wakon Tonka (God) resided there. As part of the treaty, whites, with the exception of authorized U.S. Government personnel while in the commission of official business, were forbidden to even enter the Black Hills without written permission of the Sioux.

The United States also agreed to set aside most of what is today South Dakota, Wyoming, and Montana as the "Great Sioux Reservation" and agreed that the Sioux would have full hunting and settlement rights within that area. Furthermore the Powder River area of Wyoming was closed to all white settlement forever.

In return the Sioux agreed to allow the building of railroads across the Great Plains and to allow whites to freely travel across the Great Plains while on their way to the West Coast.

What had become known as "Red Cloud's War" was over.

CHAPTER IV
AN UNEASY PEACE

The following seven years on the Great Plains were relatively peaceful for George Armstrong Custer and the 7th Cavalry. There was peace with the Cheyenne, due in large part to Custer and the 7th Cavalry, and there was peace with the Sioux now with the Fort Laramie Treaty.

During these seven years, the 7th Cavalry regiment spent a great deal of time divided up into smaller units. Custer took two companies of the regiment into Kentucky in 1871 to battle moon-shiners and the Ku Klux Klan. His efforts there proved to be quite successful. Major Marcus A Reno, the 2nd in command of the 7th, took a segment of the regiment north and assisted with the work of the International Boundary Commission as it surveyed the United States-Canada border.

During Custer's time in Kentucky another future member of the Custer family joined the 7th. Custer's sister Margaret (Maggie) had met a young, blond Civil War veteran by the name of James Calhoun in 1870 and they began "courting". During the war, Calhoun had achieved the rank of Sergeant. At the end of the war he decided to remain in the service and due to his outstanding combat record was promoted to the rank of 2nd Lieutenant.

When Calhoun started dating Maggie he began as a result to spend a great deal of time in the company of her brothers George and Tom. George liked what he saw in "Jimmi" Calhoun and pulled "strings" with the War Department and had Calhoun promoted in rank to 1st Lieutenant and assigned to the 7th.

Calhoun was very grateful. He approached George and handed him a hand written note that said "General I will never forget what you did for me here. I assure you that I will always be your supporter and that if you ever need me, you will not find me wanting."

Custer smiled back at him and responded "Jimmi I have every confidence in your abilities and I know that you won't let me down. And just remember this. I helped get you assigned to the 7th. But I would only do that for someone whose abilities I trust as after all a poor officer could get all my men and myself killed!"

Lieutenant James Calhoun would marry Margaret Custer in 1872 and would shortly become one of the key officers in the 7th Cavalry.

With the Sioux and Cheyenne seemingly subdued by the end of 1869, it finally looked like the western frontier would be opened up to peaceful settlement by whites. But there was still tension and, at times, violent clashes between whites and Indians. Part of the problem came as a result of a basic misunderstanding of Indian culture by whites. They assumed that when they signed a treaty with an Indian chief then that tribe was bound to the terms of the treaty. That wasn't in fact the case. Chiefs could only use moral persuasion to try and convince their followers to obey the treaty. They had no authority to enforce compliance.

As a result, there were numerous violations of the Fort Laramie Treaty by Indians. In particular Sitting Bull, the spiritual leader of the Hunk Papa Sioux, encouraged his followers to attack and otherwise harass railroad workers attempting to build the railways across the

Great Plains. In response to frantic complaints by railway companies, the army rushed troops to the areas involved. The 7th Cavalry was one of those units and they moved into the "Yellowstone River" area of Montana in the summer of 1873.

On August 4th of that hot summer Lieutenant Colonel Custer, along with three companies of the 7th, Cavalry made camp after a long day of riding. Custer, well aware that he was in the heart of Sioux territory, posted two, four man guard patrols. Sioux scouts spotted Custer's command and were in turn spotted by the army patrols who sounded the alarm.

Custer immediately mounted his troops, and pursued the Sioux scouts. It wasn't a "wild dash however". He left his brother Tom in the rear of his advancing unit with a company of soldiers to ensure his rear was covered. As Custer, leading his troops, closed in on a wooded area that the retreating hostiles had fled into, he slowed his advance, fearing a possible ambush. He remembered what had occurred just seven years earlier to Captain Fetterman. When he did this, an enormous force of Sioux warriors came "swarming out the woods." Just as he had figured – the Sioux had been waiting in the woods with an ambush! Badly outnumbered Custer ordered a retreat. His men withdrew past a skirmish line established by Tom Custer. The skirmish line then commenced a heavy fire into the advancing warriors stopping their advance.

With the skirmish line pouring fire into the Sioux, Custer then deployed the rest of his soldiers into a semi-circular perimeter, ensuring his troops all had clear "fields of fire" to engage the enemy.

For the next number of hours the Sioux attempted several flanking maneuvers trying to strike at Custer's men. Each time Custer coolly shifted his troops to drive off the enemy. Finally the Sioux gave up and withdrew all together. Custer had not won the battle nor had he lost. George Custer here though, exhibited a coolness under fire, and the ability to properly maneuver his troops in defensive fashion and drive off, if not defeat, a numerically superior force of hostiles.

That was a different side of him that had not been seen in the Civil War or in previous clashes with Indians. In those conflicts Custer was always on the offense and as a result had the reputation of being a very "one dimensional officer." Many of his colleagues wondered if Custer even knew how to fight a defensive battle. On the Yellowstone in 1873 he proved he could.

There was no doubt that this battle was a tremendous success for the reputation of George Armstrong Custer. He had defeated the Cheyenne at Washita, forced the remaining Cheyenne onto reservations in 1869, and now could argue had been successful against the Sioux. In the eyes of many Americans, George Armstrong Custer was now the United States Army's pre-eminent Indian fighter. The blond haired, blue- eyed, "Boy General" could not only fight and whip Confederates – he could also whip Indians. Custer had also established on the Yellowstone that, while he was indeed an aggressive commander who was always looking to attack, he was also a prudent one, who could fight a very effective defensive battle if the circumstance required him to do so.

The following year Custer again made nationwide news. The United States was in the midst of a severe economic recession, and in an effort to improve their own economic situation a group of miners and explorers, in direct violation of the 1868 Fort Laramie Treaty, had slipped into and then out of the Paha Sapa – the Black Hills. They came out alive and with news that the Black Hills were full of gold.

Desperate to try and keep a massive gold rush from breaking out which would also spark a major war with the Sioux, President Ulysses S Grant (whom Custer had served under during the Civil War when Grant commanded the Union Army of the Potomac) ordered Custer to enter the Black Hills with his entire regiment. Custer, along with the 7th, was to take along geologists and other mining experts and ascertain if indeed there was gold in the Black Hills.

The orders to Custer by President Grant were in the "gray area" in so far as the terms of the Treaty of Fort Laramie were concerned. The treaty did allow for government officials to enter the Black Hills. But the Indians claimed that when they signed they had never envisioned soldiers as "government officials" and never would have agreed to the treaty if they had known how it would be used. Grant's orders may then have been in the very strictest sense "legal", but it was hard not to argue that they violated the "spirit of the treaty."

Custer and the 7th Cavalry entered the Black Hills in the summer of 1874. They were under constant surveillance by Sioux warriors as they rode through the Black Hills, however the entire regiment of over 1,000 soldiers and civilians was simply too strong for the Indians to take on in a battle. They were furious at the invasion of their holy land but powerless to stop it.

After six weeks of extensive exploration in the Black Hills, the 7th Cavalry emerged, and Custer reported to Washington that there was gold in the Black Hills.

Intense pressure now mounted on President Grant and the rest of the U.S. Government to open up the Black Hills for gold mining. The country was gripped by a severe recession, and that gold located in the Black Hills would help in the nation's economic recovery, many economic experts argued. A significant portion of Members of Congress agreed. Grant, to be fair, argued that under the terms of the Treaty of Fort Laramie the U.S. government was powerless to allow mining. And in order to prevent a major war from breaking out as miners began entering the Black Hills illegally, Grant ordered the 7th Cavalry to "police the area" and arrest anyone they found entering the Black Hills illegally.

Custer and his troops did try very hard to obey the orders of the President. It was an impossible task in this age before the invention of modern radio communications to coordinate troop movements, and/or the use of aircraft and satellites for surveillance. The area was simply too big, and there were too few troops to be successful.

President Grant realized what an impossible position he had put Custer and his troops in and decided to follow the general feelings of Congress and popular opinion. And that was to find a way to get the gold in the Black Hills into the hands of Americans. After all, as many Americans were saying, the Sioux were simply uncivilized savages, and had no use for the gold there. As far as Grant was concerned, the Sioux didn't vote so it would not matter politically to him if he upset them. The consensus was that the gold rightly belonged to the American people, regardless of what the terms of the 1868 Treaty of Fort Laramie stated.

Emissaries were sent from Washington to meet with Sioux chiefs and get the Sioux to sell the Black Hills to the U.S. Government. The response the government negotiators received was not what they wanted to hear. It was the same they would have received if they asked the Pope how much he would be willing to sell the Vatican for, or a Rabbi what he would sell the Western Wall in Jerusalem for. In other words, the Black Hills where not for sale at any price. Crazy Horse summed up the Sioux's position by stating "One does not sell the land upon which one walks."

Congress and the Grant Administration were furious. In their eyes and experience, everything was for sale. Everything had its price, and the Indians had better realize it. In the late fall of 1875, Congress announced that the Sioux's actions on the Great Plains, directed towards the building of the railways, had violated the terms of the Treaty of Fort Laramie and as such the treaty as a whole was null and void. Congress was purchasing the Black Hills for the sum of $6,000,000.00 (they picked that dollar figure, not the Sioux).

Furthermore all Sioux and Cheyenne not currently on reservations had to be so by January 31, 1876, or they would be considered hostile and turned over to the army to be dealt with. In the eyes of many, war was imminent.

Very few of the "hostiles" actually heard the ultimatum from Congress. After all, these were the days before radios and television, so news travelled very slowly across the vast distances of the Great Plains. Those that did receive the ultimatum had no intention of making a long trek to a reservation during the winter. They were settled into their winter camps and were not going anywhere.

Once the deadline had passed the Army began to prepare for war. For most of the officers involved, this upcoming campaign would probably be their last opportunity to advance their careers through Indian combat. Clearly in their eyes, the "writing was on the wall" in so far as who was going to win the struggle for land on the western frontier. White civilization was not going to be held back.

CHAPTER V
THE MARCH TO WAR

At Fort Abraham Lincoln in Dakota Territory (now modern day North Dakota), where the 7th Cavalry was now based, George Armstrong Custer was making preparations. In the past, his regiment had been rarely operated as an intact unit. It was now together, and Custer had no doubts that it would triumph over the Indians when it met them.

As the U.S. Army began its war preparations, another type of drama was gripping Washington that spring. Congress had launched an investigation into the conduct of Secretary of War William Belknap. It was alleged that Belknap was involved in serious corruption. The army fell under the jurisdiction of the War Department, and as such was heavily involved in the outcome of this investigation.

One of the areas being investigated was granting of licenses for sutlers. The sutler was a merchant (granted a license by the War Department) who set up operations at various army forts and outposts. It was from the sutlers that soldiers could purchase clothing, tobacco, liquor, etc. It was a source of great anger among soldiers that the prices sutlers charged for their goods was usually significantly higher than those charged by merchants in nearby towns. When soldiers in response took to shopping in town, the sutlers complained to the War Department, who then issued an edict that the soldiers were to confine their business to that of the sutler.

Custer sent various written complaints to the War Department over this, and to various Democrats in both the Senate and House of Representatives. (Custer was an ardent Democrat.) As Custer was making preparations for the 7th's campaign, he received a telegram ordering him to travel immediately to Washington to testify before what was being called the "Belknap Commission." He was furious at the interruption.

"Libbie" he yelled, when the offending telegram arrived. "God, damn it look at this" he exclaimed shaking the offending piece of paper in his hand. "Congress first tells me the Indians have to be on reservations by the end of January or they'd be considered hostile and turned over to the army. I am getting ready for a campaign against them just as Congress said to, and now they want me to leave my regiment as we are preparing and come to Washington for some foolish committee hearing. What the hell is wrong with them?"

Libbie Custer was very familiar with her high-strung husband's ways. "Now calm down, Autie", she said. "For years you have railed against the War Department and the way the sutlers take advantage of your men. Now you have a real chance to do something about it. They really seem to be looking into this and who would have more influence on them than you?"

George Custer, while still angry, calmed down. As usual Libbie made sense. "You're right", he answered. "I'll go there and get it over with as fast as possible and get back here. The 7th won't leave without me after all. But damn it, this is just bad timing."

"That's the right attitude," she beamed. "Now get to Washington and make a difference! And while you are there make sure you spend time with some Democrats and let it be known that some day the Custers may like to live in the White House!"

Autie smiled at the last remark. He had not made it public but as a long time supporter of the Democratic Party he had dreamed of becoming President. And it wasn't a far-fetched dream seeing as General Ulysses S Grant, whom Custer had served under during the Civil War, was the current President (albeit as a Republican).

"Libbie", he said. "Rest assured I will be doing that while I am there. And just think. If I can whip the hostiles before the Democratic Convention this summer, people would be clamoring for me to get the Democratic nomination if I made it clear I was interested. Grant is tired and his administration is corrupt. I can whip him in an election as easily as I can whip those Indians."

The evening before leaving for Washington he called his officers together. He looked around the room and his heart was full of pride. "No other regiment in the army can boast of the leadership strength like the 7th has" he thought.

He looked at younger brother Tom, now a Captain and the commanding officer of Company C. "Autie" had stated many times that in his opinion Tom was a superior soldier to himself and should in fact be the General. Tom, while very flattered, was completely devoted to his brother and utterly loyal. There was no jealousy on Tom Custer's part towards his older brother.

Next to Tom was Lieutenant William Cooke. Cooke was one of Custer's most loyal and capable officers and served in the 7th as Custer's Adjutant (or "assistant"). It was Cooke's role to be Custer's "eyes and ears" in the regiment, and to be by his side at all times during combat. One of the highlights of Cooke's life was when he brought Custer home to his home town of Hamilton, Ontario for a visit. There was no mission that Custer could assign to Cooke that would be too great for the Canadian officer to undertake for his commanding officer. Cooke was also very well liked among the other officers and enlisted men of the 7th Cavalry. He was soft-spoken, and surprisingly very sensitive. But beneath that layer of true sensibility, he was a tough, loyal, and very capable officer.

There was Lieutenant James "Jimmi' Calhoun, "the Blond Adonis" of the 7th Cavalry and commander of Company L. Calhoun was tall, blond haired and, unlike many army officers, totally devoted to his wife (Maggie Custer) and thus was not one to chase women as many of his fellow officers did. Calhoun had by now proven himself as a very able officer, popular with all members of the regiment.

Custer's eyes now landed on Lieutenant Algernon "Fresh" Smith, commander of Company E. Lieutenant Smith, a brave, competent officer, had a crippled arm as a result of a Civil War wound and should have been released from the army as a result. Custer, however, fought successfully to keep Smith due to Smith's complete loyalty to Custer.

Next he looked at Captain George Yates, a fellow officer from Monroe, Michigan, and commander of Company F. The two had served together in the Civil War and Custer had arranged for him to be assigned to the 7th in 1866. They were close personal friends and few were more loyal to George Armstrong Custer than was George Yates.

He then gazed upon Captain Myles Keogh, commander of Company I. Keogh had been born in Ireland, and as a young man had served in the Papal Guard protecting Pope Pius IX, at the Vatican. In 1862, he resigned his commission with the Papal Guard and moved to the United States with the purpose of serving in the Union Army during the Civil War. Keogh served with great distinction during this conflict and after the war was awarded with a commission in the 7th Cavalry. Captain Keogh was a well-respected and personally well-liked officer in the regiment, although he could be prone to heavy drinking and more than the occasional touch of melancholy. He was fiercely loyal to George Custer.

Custer than looked Captain Thomas Weir, commander of D Company in the eyes. Weir was another of the "Custer Clan." Weir, a very capable officer, was completely and utterly loyal to Custer. If Custer commanded him to do so, Weir would without question or hesitation follow his commanding officer to the gates of hell and beyond.

Major Marcus Reno and Captain Frederick Benteen were sitting together, and Custer briefly looked at them. Both Reno and Benteen had served with distinction and honor in the Civil War. Benteen joined the 7th in January 1867, and had commanded Company H since then. He had narrowly avoided being killed at the Battle of Washita after his horse was shot and killed from underneath him. Benteen and Custer personally despised one another. However, Custer respected Benteen as a tough, capable officer and never expressed any doubts that Benteen would carry out any orders assigned to him. Reno joined the 7th in late 1868, just a month after the Washita battle. He was second in command in the regiment after Custer. Like Benteen, Reno was not one of the so-called "Custer Clan" as officers such as Tom Custer, Calhoun, Smith, and Keogh, among others, were called. While he didn't despise Custer in the same way as did Benteen, he didn't have a warm relationship with him either. Both Reno and Custer tended to be very formal with each other, and only spoke to each other when there was official business to be discussed.

There were other officers present such as Captains Myles Moylen and Thomas French, Lieutenants Donald McIntosh (who like William Cooke was Canadian born, having being born in Montreal to a white father and Iroquois mother), Edward Godfrey, George Wallace, and Benjamin Hodgson, to name a few.

The room became quiet as Custer began to speak.

"Thank you for coming, gentlemen. Tomorrow I will be travelling to Washington. I have been called to testify before Congress. There is an investigation being conducted into the affairs of Secretary of War Belknap and they wish for me to speak about the sutler issue. I will certainly impress upon them the hardships our men suffer as a result of the greed of the sutlers.

While I am away I expect that the 7th will continue to prepare for war. And let me assure you all that we are going to war. And we will whip Sitting Bull and the Sioux so badly no Indian will ever dare to leave a reservation again. I am convinced that this campaign will be the final one ever against Indians, and the 7th will go down in history as the regiment that brought peace to the west. There is plenty of glory waiting for us if we do our jobs properly. And I have no doubt that we all will."

Benteen spoke up. "General", he began. "Will it just be our regiment going into action or will we be supported by other troops?"

"Captain that is a good question. My understanding is that we will be cooperating with forces commanded by Generals Crook and Terry as well as Colonel Gibbon. How closely we will operate with them I do not know as of yet. That will be something I am sure I will find out in Washington. And when I know, rest assured all of you will know."

After more general conversation, the meeting broke up and Custer started on his way to Washington the next day.

The journey to Washington wasn't easy. He traveled via horse, stagecoach, and finally train before he made it to the nation's capital. When he got there, he was first immersed in meetings with General Phil Sheridan, General George Crook, General Alfred Terry, and Colonel John Gibbon regarding the upcoming campaign against the Sioux and Cheyenne. There was some superb military talent gathered at these planning meetings. General Sheridan was among the highest ranking and most experienced of all American army officers. He had recalled Custer from his suspension back in 1868 and turned him loose against the Cheyenne that year. He would remain in Washington with overall command responsibility for this campaign.

General George Crook had been an outstanding Civil War combat leader, and had then parlayed that success into great triumph fighting the Apache Indians in the Southwest. The Apache had wreaked havoc across the Southwestern United States and Mexico. Truth be told, while George Custer was better known by the American public as an Indian fighter, George Crook actually had more experience and more success fighting Indians than did Custer. The advantages Custer had over Crook in this theater of operations were experience in fighting Plains Indians and knowledge of the terrain they'd be marching into. Crook's experience, again, had come against the Apache in modern day Arizona.

Colonel John Gibbon was both an experienced Civil War veteran and Indian fighter. He was known to the Indians as "No Hip Bone" due to a severe limp he had as a result of a Civil War wound. Gibbon wasn't a flashy officer like Custer. He was quiet and reserved, but he got the job done and was very well respected within the military.

General Alfred Terry was another Civil War veteran and was also a lawyer. He was superbly educated, very intelligent, and a thoughtful, even sensitive man. Many thought that General Terry might in fact be the nicest man in the entire U.S. military. It would be General Terry who would be in overall command of the campaign, in the field and he would report directly back to General Sheridan on the progress the troops were making.

Terry, unlike braggarts like William Fetterman, was very cognizant of the fact that fighting Indians was dramatically different from that of fighting Confederates. He planned on relying on the Indian fighting skills and experience that Crook, Custer, and Gibbon had in planning his military actions on this campaign.

The plan, as it was laid out, would have Crook's forces marching northwards from Fort Fetterman in Wyoming Territory. Gibbon's forces would march east from Fort Ellis in Dakota Territory while Custer's would march west from Fort Abraham Lincoln. This would be the single largest operation ever launched by the United States Army against the Plains Indians. It was expected that Crook's forces, being the farthest away, would attempt to coordinate their action with those of Gibbon and Terry (Custer being included with Terry). It was understood that Crook might have to operate individually if circumstances warranted it and he was unable to get direction from Terry.

During these meetings, Custer raised a concern with all present.

"Gentlemen." he began. "I have to say I am very concerned with the Springfield carbine my men and indeed all the cavalry troopers have been equipped with. I agree that it is accurate and has excellent range. The problem we are having is combining the Springfield with the copper jacketed cartridges we have been issued. Copper is much softer then brass which is normally used for cartridges. We are finding that during use, as the Springfield heats up, the copper shells get even softer with the heat and the extractor on the Springfield can rip the lip off the copper cartridge, leaving it jammed in the weapon. Gentleman this could be a recipe for disaster in battle! Add to this, I am hearing stories that many of the hostiles we are going after are equipped with Henry and Winchester repeating rifles. The Springfield, as we all know, is a single shot weapon. I do not look forward to sending my men into battle armed with single shot carbines against a force equipped with repeating rifles. We will be outgunned right away. And that is the best scenario – that is, assuming the Springfields are not jamming. And our experience in the field is that they will jam."

General Sheridan responded. "Armstrong, I understand your concerns, and within this room I share some of them. We should be using brass cartridge cases. However, copper is cheaper and that is why the army went that route. I disagreed with that. As for the weapon, well the Springfield is a good weapon. It has a better range than any repeating rifle the hostiles will have and better stopping power. That being said, your troops will be at a disadvantage if the hostiles are heavily equipped with repeating arms. And the important word here is 'if.' My belief is, the amount of repeaters that the hostiles actually do have is exaggerated. If the hostiles do fight, I don't believe that the amount of repeating arms that they actually do have will prove to be a major problem for your troops."

"I'll also point out that your men do have the option of purchasing their own weapons. They don't have to use the Springfield if they don't want to. They can buy and use whatever rifle they choose to. And if they buy their own rifle they can also buy their own ammunition. They don't need to use army issued ammunition."

Custer always had the greatest of respect for Phil Sheridan and chose his words carefully in response.

"General", he said. "I certainly respect your opinion but have to say I surely hope that you are correct, sir, in so far as how many repeating arms the hostiles have. As for purchasing their own weapons, well technically speaking you are, of course, correct sir. American soldiers have always had that option. Realistically speaking, however, their levels of pay are so low that few of them can actually make use of that option."

Sheridan smiled back at Custer. "Armstrong", he responded. "I don't set the pay levels for soldiers. Congress does that. Nor do I select the weapons the army chooses to buy. I make do with what they give me or I buy my own. I'd suggest to you here that you are complaining to the wrong person. In so far as what the hostiles are armed with, well even if I am wrong I have every confidence that you and the mighty 7th Cavalry will whip the hostiles soundly, regardless of what arms they have."

"We won't let you down sir," Custer answered.

During this time in Washington, Custer also had to make several appearances before Congress to testify in the investigation over corruption in the War Department. His testimony proved devastating to Secretary of War William Belknap and to Orville Grant, brother of President Ulysses Grant. Custer's testimony directly implicated Belknap and Orville Grant in the alleged sale of sutler licenses, and President Grant was outraged.

Custer had not taken care in how he presented his evidence, and had provided few verifiable facts to support what he was saying. What he said may have been accurate, however, without detailed facts to support it, it appeared that he was attacking some of the most prominent members of the Grant Administration with nothing but "hearsay" evidence.

After his testimony, Custer traveled to Philadelphia and New York on personal business, and was then summoned back to Washington for further testimony. There he found that his earlier testimony had created a true "firestorm" of controversy. General William Sherman, the highest ranking officer in the United States Army, indicated in a letter to General Terry that Custer's testimony had been so enraging to Grant that nobody in the army would dare support him.

In an effort to try to repair the damage he had done, Custer requested a personal meeting with Grant. However, the President refused to meet with him. In total frustration, and eager to get back to his regiment, Custer left Washington on May 3 onboard a train for Chicago. Grant, while not willing to meet with Custer, seemed to enjoy leaving the "Boy General" in limbo in Washington. He exploded when he found out Custer had left Washington without direct orders to do so. He ordered General Sherman to "intercept" Custer, and not allow him to proceed back to Fort Abraham Lincoln. Grant also ordered Major Marcus Reno to take command of the 7th Cavalry on the upcoming campaign.

Sherman passed Grant's orders to General Sheridan to carry out. Custer was stopped en route to Chicago and was ordered to proceed immediately to Fort Snelling, Minnesota, and "hold there." Custer was inconsolable upon hearing Grant's orders. He had traveled to Washington as the "Boy General", America's greatest Indian fighter and in the back of his mind a candidate for the Presidency. Now his military career was in tatters. His beloved 7th Cavalry would be marching off on its greatest campaign without him, and it appeared he had burned every bridge he had in the army and government.

While at Fort Snelling, Custer met with General Terry. In a scene which, years later, Terry seemed uncomfortable reciting, Custer, on bent knees and with tears in his eyes, begged Terry to intercede on his behalf with the President. Terry respected Custer's professional abilities and wanted him on the campaign. However, he knew he had to "tread softly" as President Grant was obviously livid with Custer, and Terry didn't want to place his own career in jeopardy.

Terry suggested that Custer write a very carefully worded letter to the President asking him to reconsider, and Terry would add a personal note of his own. Custer did exactly that, writing a very heartfelt letter to President Grant asking him in part to spare him the humiliation of watching his regiment march into danger while he was left behind. General Terry added a personal note indicating that while he respected and would follow the President's orders, he did feel that Custer's services on the campaign would be very valuable if he was allowed to take part.

When Grant received the correspondence, he cursed under his

breath. By now he simply couldn't stand Custer, and was beside himself in rage over the damage done to his administration by Custer's hearsay testimony before Congress. On the other hand, as a former military officer himself, he knew there was no better officer in the entire United States Army to turn loose on the Indians trail than George Armstrong Custer. Add to that, the personal note from General Terry carried a lot of weight with Grant. The President remembered his own days in the army when he'd curse the decisions made by politicians who he felt knew nothing about military affairs. He wasn't going to do the same to Terry. If Terry wanted Custer, he could have him. But, in his response back to the two men, President Grant made it very clear that, although Custer was reinstated as commanding officer of the 7th Cavalry, the 7th would serve under the overall command of General Terry who would ride with the 7th.

Custer was ecstatic at his reinstatement and he, along with General Terry, hurried to Fort Abraham Lincoln on May 10, 1876, to get the 7th Cavalry "on the move." A week of frantic activity followed as the 7th began to prepare to move out. Wagons had to be packed, horses checked to ensure they were healthy, weapons cleaned and readied, etc. Convinced as he was that this would be largest and, in all likelihood, final campaign against the Indians, Custer wanted to ensure as many members of his family as possible would share in the glory. Along with Tom and Lieutenant Calhoun, his youngest brother Boston and nephew Arthur Reed would join them employed as civilian aides.

During that final, frantic week of furious preparation numerous scouting reports arrived at the fort. The reports all stated the same thing. Hundreds, maybe even thousands, of Sioux and Cheyenne were leaving their reservations and heading west towards Montana Territory. If the 7th was going into battle, it would be facing numerous foes.

On the morning of May 17, 1876, the 7th Cavalry marched out of

Fort Abraham Lincoln. In the days leading up to the departure an unexplainable sense of foreboding, almost gloom and fear, permeated the fort and its inhabitants. Annie Yates, wife of Captain George Yates, had a disturbing dream in which she saw Custer shot in the head by an Indian. She mentioned it to Custer who used humor to try and reassure her. Usually, due to Custer's natural exuberance, the fort was a lively place and the mood was light. Not this time. There was a sense among the soldiers, their wives, and children, that this would be a very different campaign. Nobody could explain why – it was just there. It rained heavily in the days leading up to the regiments departure and that only added to the sense of impending doom.

The regiment, 1,200 strong, marched out into a thick fog that blanketed the fort and the surrounding area that morning as the regimental band played "The Girl I Left Behind Me." The soldiers leaving Fort Abraham Lincoln that day did not look like cavalry troopers as depicted by Hollywood. They were not clad in sharp blue uniforms as seen in the movies. Most wore army issued trousers and boots, but instead of army blouses and hats, they wore flannel shirts, and whatever hats they personally preferred. Custer was wearing a white buckskin outfit with a wide brimmed white hat. Unless they bought their own personal firearms, each soldier was equipped with a single-shot Model 1873 Springfield carbine and a .45 caliber Colt Army revolver. Most troopers also carried some form of hunting knife. Officers traditionally bought their own firearms. For this campaign, Custer was carrying a Remington sporting rifle and two English Webley revolvers.

While in the field, the army didn't eat extravagant meals. In so far as meat went, there was heavily salted bacon to eat. Otherwise the only meat came from any wildlife a soldier was able to shoot while in the field. Hardtack, a type of bland, flour-based biscuit, was a staple of a soldier's diet. It was usually rock-hard, (some of Custer's troops had rations of hardtack that had been in storage since the Civil War!) and lacked a great deal of nutrition, however it did fill a stomach. To drink, soldiers would usually brew coffee over an open fire. Each soldier carried at least one canteen which would be filled, usually with water, but if he had paid a visit recently to the sutler, then sometimes with whiskey.

Custer arranged for Libbie and Maggie Calhoun to join the march for the first day. That morning, as the 7th marched and the sun burned the fog off, Libber Custer saw an astonishing site. A mirage, created by the suns rays reflecting off the fog, showed about half the regiment marching into the sky. It was a scene that chilled her to the bone and strengthened her own feelings that her husband's regiment was destined to meet with some form of disaster.

That first night the 7th camped along the Heart River. It was there that Custer ordered the regimental Paymaster to pay his troops. He had held off doing so earlier as he didn't want his troopers heading into the bars and brothels of nearby Bismarck. With their pay in hand now, the soldiers could still buy whiskey from the sutler that would accompany them. However, Custer didn't have to worry about his troops disappearing into town and not returning.

The following morning there was a heartrending scene as Libbie and Maggie Calhoun left to return to Fort Abraham Lincoln. Libbie in particular was inconsolable as she headed back. She couldn't shake the feeling that she would never again see her husband alive.

The ladies rode back to the fort with a military escort accompanying them while the bulk of the 7th moved westwards. For the next two weeks, the 7th battled some of the most bizarre weather they had ever come across on the Great Plains. Days of heavy rain erupted, turning the terrain into a quagmire, which slowed the wagons, and as a result the entire regiment, to a crawl. Despite the best efforts of the powerful army horses pulling them, many times the wagons were completely immobilized in mud. When that occurred, soldiers were forced to dismount and aid in pushing the wagons until they were free.

When the rains finally stopped, the regiment was then blasted by a final eruption of winter. For two days snow fell and the temperatures plummeted. Soldiers who were already miserable due to their sodden clothing, blankets and tents, were shivering in the intense cold. Sleep was almost impossible, as the soldiers couldn't remove their boots at night. The boots when wet would swell making them impossible to put back on. Their clothes, tents, and blankets were soaked. Outside of huddling by a fire there was no way to get dry and/or warm.

When the cold ended the summer began with a fury. Temperatures rose rapidly, the skies cleared of all clouds, and the sun beat down on the column without mercy. As the temperatures climbed, the ground dried up and the air became thick with heavy dust kicked up by the horses and wagons. Huge horse and deer flies began swarming among the soldiers and horses leaving bloody wounds on all exposed flesh. The soldiers responded by tying bandanas around their faces, leaving only their eyes exposed. They dabbed coal oil on the bandannas to drive the flies away. The problem with that was that the coal oil smelled so bad that it was questionable what was worse – the flies or the smell of coal oil!

The sun was so intense that any exposed flesh soon became badly sunburned. A soldier who didn't tie a bandana around his face or at least have a full beard and mustache soon found himself with lips that were so burned by the sun that they bled whenever they tried to talk or even smile. Those who tried to drink the whiskey in their canteens cursed as the raw liquor seared their scorched bloody lips.

These were the days before modern hygiene techniques. The cotton and wool clothing/uniforms worn by the soldiers had already been soaked in rain, snow, and were now drenched in sweat. The only way to bathe was if they camped near a river and soldiers took the time to wash in that. Actually washing their clothes was practically impossible. The best they could do was soak them in river water. There was no such thing as antiperspirants or deodorants in those days, and when you added in the smells of the animals, the stench coming from the army columns would travel for miles.

As May ended and June began, the 7th Cavalry was moving through territory few if any whites had entered. They were now deep in the heart of hostile Sioux and Cheyenne territory, and all around the mounted troopers were signs of the enemy. The hoof marks of massive pony herds were evident along with the deep gauges left in the land by teepee poles being dragged as Indian villages moved west – away from the reservations. Massive fire and teepee circles from where the hostiles had made camps left the cavalry troopers feeling very "somber." The Arikara and Crow scouts employed by Custer were telling each other that never in their lives had they seen such large trails and campsites. The soldiers themselves were no dummies – they saw the evidence and knew they were not going to be facing a few isolated villages. They were in for a massive struggle.

The three U.S. Army columns were marching towards the largest encampments of Native Indians in North American history. Earlier that spring, Sitting Bull called for a gathering of the entire Sioux Nation along with their Cheyenne allies. Never before had all the Sioux gathered together. Hunk Papa, Oglala, Santee, Miniconjou, Blackfoot, all the Sioux were heading for, what would later become modern day, Montana. The Cheyenne were also leaving reservations in droves to join their traditional allies. Sitting Bull had a vision that spring of many soldiers "falling into" Sioux and Cheyenne villages. He took that to mean that there would be an immense battle fought between the Sioux and Cheyenne and the army, and that the Indians would emerge victorious. He told the Sioux and Cheyenne "let the soldiers come and find us. This time we will not run from them. This time we will kill them all."

As they continued into hostile Indian territory, the scouts at times lost their bearings in the rough, broken terrain. On two different occasions, Custer personally took over plotting the course of the regiment and both times led them "back on track," leading Terry to comment "Only Custer could have pulled us through that." Alfred Terry was simply in awe of Custer's skills in the field that were far and away better than his own.

On another occasion Custer, who regularly rode ahead of even the scouts, took off far in advance of the column accompanied by brothers Tom and Boston. George and Tom then slipped away from Boston and hid amongst some rocks. When young Boston began a search for his older brothers, both George and Tom began firing their rifles over his head and making Indian war cries. Convinced he had blundered into a Sioux war party, Boston Custer frantically put his spurs to his horse and began a frenzied ride back towards the main army column. Laughing all the way, both George and Tom Custer had to ride hard to catch their younger brother and prevent him from passing on erroneous information.

On June 15th, the column bivouacked for the night. Eager to keep moving and always conscious of how fast the Plains Indians could break camp and escape, Custer now ordered all his men to box up their sabers and leave them at their current camp site which would be known as "Camp Supply." The saber was a useful cavalry weapon in the Civil War when opposing soldiers fought at close quarters. Plains Indians however rarely came close enough to a trooper where a saber could be used. The cavalry saber was heavy and by leaving them behind Custer felt it was one less item that would slow his men down.

He also ordered the regimental band to remain at Camp Supply and had their horses distributed throughout the regiment. If the 7th went into battle on this campaign, they would not do so with the tune of "Garry Owen" playing in the background by their band.

That evening Custer and Terry met. They had been receiving regular updates via mounted scouts regarding the progress of Colonel Gibbon's column. But to date there had been no news or reports from Crook. It was almost as if he had dropped off the face of the earth and General Terry was concerned. He and Crook did not personally care for one another (odd in that Alfred Terry was so well liked personally throughout the military) but Terry didn't believe that personal feelings would prompt Crook's unusual silence.

That same week, Terry sent Major Reno ahead of the column on a scouting mission with six companies of the 7th. Custer was furious at Terry for not allowing him to personally lead the scouting mission. Reno discovered a trail that his scouts informed him would take him directly to the hostiles' village. In a move that further infuriated Custer, Reno turned his forces around and didn't follow the trail to ascertain the exact position of the Indian village. When Reno returned, Custer exploded at him for his failure to follow up and possibly strike the village when he had the opportunity. (Which is exactly what he, Custer, would have done if he had been in command of the scouting mission.)

CHAPTER VI
BLOOD IS DRAWN

Two days after the 7th bivouacked at Camp Supply, General Crook and his column made contact with the hostiles. Crook had come into this campaign very confident that he could whip the Sioux and Cheyenne. He had soundly beaten Confederates in the Civil War, and had thoroughly humbled the Apaches in the Southwest. He knew in his heart that he, George Crook, was America's pre-eminent Indian fighter, not George Custer. He had proven that with the Apaches and he didn't feel the Sioux and their Cheyenne allies would be much of a challenge for him.

It was true that Crook didn't care for General Terry, and while he sent regular dispatches back via mounted scouts to General Sheridan in Washington, he made no effort to contact General Terry or Colonel Gibbon. Crook was determined to single-handedly bring peace to the Great Plains by crushing Sitting Bull, and he didn't want to be bothered by having General Terry "looking over his shoulder."

On Saturday morning, June 17, 1876, Crook's column was marching northward along the Rosebud Creek in Montana Territory. His men were tired. They had marched 35 miles the day before in the sizzling heat and had been up since reveille was sounded at 3am.

Crook halted the column at 8am to offer a brief rest to the men and their animals. He was deep inside Indian territory, but so far his scouts had seen no signs that any hostiles were close. As a result, Crook made no defensive preparations with his military forces, although he did direct his scouts to positions on the bluffs surrounding his position.

What Crook didn't know was that his column had been under surveillance for some time by Sioux and Cheyenne scouts. Once he reached the Rosebud Valley, Sitting Bull and Crazy Horse decided he had come close enough. It was time to teach the "wasicu" (the Sioux term for whites) a lesson in the power of the mighty Sioux and Cheyenne nations!

Shortly after the column halted, the resting soldiers were startled to hear rapid exchanges of gunfire from the bluffs. The gunfire continued to grow more intense and some of the scouts galloped into the soldiers' position screaming "Lakota, Lakota." Other scouts remained on the bluffs, hotly engaged by attacking Sioux and Cheyenne warriors.

Crook was initially shocked. He had over 1,000 soldiers and civilians under his command, and never before in history had a column the size of his been attacked by hostiles. It just didn't happen! However he was too good an officer not to respond. He began to deploy his command, ordering his forces to seize the high ground north and south of the creek valley he was in. He had to control the high ground, otherwise the hostiles could pour fire down upon his men – just as what occurred 10 years earlier with Captain William Fetterman. To aid in this, he ordered Captain Anson Mills to take six companies of the 3rd Cavalry Regiment (which was part of Crook's column) and charge the attacking Sioux and Cheyenne warriors. This tactic worked, and the hostiles withdrew before Captain Mills' charge.

As this was occurring, more hostiles attacked the rear of Crook's command and Crook ordered his second in command, Lieutenant Colonel William Royall to disperse that threat. In the savage fighting that resulted, Royall's force was almost cut off and destroyed and Royall was forced to withdraw back to the main command.

Crook's other deployments succeeded in gaining the bluffs surrounding the valley. However, much to the shock of the army, the warriors didn't withdraw as history indicted they would. Directed by Crazy Horse, who rode amongst the various warriors, they continued to harass the soldiers, firing from a distance at them, and launching lightning quick assaults on army positions. Crook, always calm and cool, would respond by launching cavalry counter-assaults breaking up the warriors' attacks. The Sioux and Cheyenne, however, were always able to gallop away before the cavalry troopers could catch them. Crook's men poured volley after volley of concentrated gunfire into the attacking warriors, while the hostiles responded with their own barrage of rifle fire and volleys of arrows.

The battle raged non-stop for over six hours, with casualties mounting on both sides. The Rosebud Valley was thick with gun smoke and the dust kicked up by galloping horses. Finally the hostiles began a withdrawal from the field of battle that left Crook and his forces in control of the valley and the surrounding bluffs.

Army doctrine then and today dictated that Crook should pursue the withdrawing hostiles after he drove them from the battlefield. The United States Army has always taught its officers that if you drive an enemy from the battlefield you continue to pursue them until you either re-engage them in battle and destroy them, or they surrender. These were the expectations placed on George Crook after what became known as "The Battle of the Rosebud." Instead in a startling – even shocking – choice Crook made the decision to withdraw. His reasoning was simple. His forces had expended over 25,000 rounds of ammunition in the battle and he had suffered casualties. He felt he had neither the manpower nor the ammunition to successfully pursue the hostiles and defeat them in battle once he did catch them. His wounded needed medical care and he couldn't be dragging them around the Great Plains chasing after Crazy Horse.

This decision of Crooks' was roundly criticized but his next decision was even more shocking. He made no effort at all, to send word of what occurred to either General Terry or Colonel Gibbon. The fact that the hostiles had attacked a column the size of General Crook's was without historical precedent in North America and Terry and Gibbon may have rethought their plans if they had received word from Crook on what had occurred. If nothing else it would have provided "iron-clad proof" that the hostiles they were pursuing were well-armed, well lead, and in an incredibly furious frame of mind.

Instead Crook remained silent. (To the day he died, George Crook never gave a satisfactory answer as to why he acted in this manner.) After withdrawing from the Rosebud Valley, Crook then halted his forces, set up defensive positions, and spent a number of days hunting and fishing. His behavior baffled his officers who simply could not understand it. It was almost as if General Crook, the "great Apache fighter" had been completely un-nerved by the ferocity of the Sioux and Cheyenne warriors and he withdrew into himself. That may be another possible reason why he didn't pursue them from the Rosebud battlefield. Perhaps he feared what would occur if he caught them? Crook was also well aware of just how close to disaster his column had come. If his scouts had not engaged Crazy Horse's warriors as aggressively as they did, the hostiles would have hit his unprepared command like a hurricane. It was the tremendous bravery of his Indian scouts that gave Crook the time to get his men deployed and then engage the enemy.

For the rest of his life George Crook would claim the Rosebud as a victory pointing out he had driven the enemy from the field of battle. In technical terms he was probably correct and there was no doubt in anyone's mind that he did a fine job as a battlefield commander during the actual Rosebud battle. He remained cool and in control during the battle and did a superb job properly deploying his forces to meet the attacks from the Sioux and Cheyenne. His later actions, though, nullified that victory.

Wednesday June 21, 1876 – Late Afternoon
Montana Territory – Yellow Stone River
Aboard the steamship Far West

General Alfred E. Terry called the meeting to order on board the steamship "Far West." The ship had sailed up the Yellowstone River carrying mail and other military directives for General Terry. When it departed it would carry written correspondence from Terry and his other officers back east. Gathered around him were the senior officers of his column, including General Custer and those of Colonel Gibbon's column. The two columns had now rendezvoused together.

Before Terry began to speak, there was much conversation amongst the officers over the complete lack of any news from General Crook. "Where was he?" was the unanswered question.

"Gentlemen" Terry began. "As we all know there has been no word from General Crook. I am beginning to fear the worst as I cannot imagine why, if he was operating according to plan, we have not received any word from him. As of now we will operate on the assumption that Crook will not be in support of our operation."

When Terry stated that, there were some muttered comments and nodding of heads among the gathered officers. They too were confused and worried at the utter lack of communication emanating from Crook.

Terry then went on: "The scouts tell me we are closing in on the largest encampment of Indians ever seen here on the plains. We have all seen the trails they are leaving as they move west. I believe the scouts are correct in so far as the size of the camps go. They feel the hostiles will be setting up camp in or around the Little Big Horn Valley. From what we know that is an area rich with grass, trees, and water. A perfect area for the hostiles to graze their ponies. The rivers are supposed to be full of fish so it makes sense they would set up camp there. We are about a five-day ride from there right now according to the scouts."

He then outlined his plan plotting the proposed routes the columns would follow on a map laid out on a table.

"Tomorrow, General Custer will take his 7th Cavalry and follow that trail. The 7th will not bring any wagons along. All reserve ammunition and other supplies will be carried on mules in a pack train.[5] The 7th will follow the trail south along the Rosebud until reaching the border of Wyoming Territory. They will then begin a sweep west towards the Little Big Horn Valley, blocking any escape of the hostiles while doing so. Meanwhile, I will stay with Colonel Gibbon's column, and we will move on a northerly route along the Big Horn River and rendezvous with the 7th on or about June 26th in the Little Big Horn Valley. I anticipate that Custer will attack the hostiles from the south and as the hostiles flee to the north we will be in a blocking position to prevent that."

Alfred Terry had earlier told Custer what the plan was. With Terry's words out in the open a grim smile appeared on George Armstrong

---

[5] General George Crook made famous use of mules and pack trains during his campaigns against the Apache. He'd pack all his forces' reserve ammunition, food, tools, etc on mules as opposed to wagons, and found that his columns moved much more quickly and efficiently. He especially found that mules could travel or access areas that wagons could not.

Custer's face. He had been "itching" to break loose from Terry on this campaign and strike out against the hostiles with just the 7th. Now he would have that opportunity.

Terry made some further comments and then opened up the floor for discussion. Colonel Gibbon, had been overly cautious on his own march from Fort Ellis. (Some would argue he did his best to avoid any contact with potential hostiles). He was deeply concerned that the aggressive Custer, having being turned loose, may run into some serious trouble if he encountered the hostiles "on his own." As such he made Custer an offer:

"General, to aid you in your scouting mission up the Rosebud, I'd like to offer you four of my cavalry companies. They will give you some more badly needed strength if you should run into the hostiles. You may need them if the hostiles are as numerous as our scouts think that they are."

General Terry interjected, "Now Custer, that is a very generous offer and I believe you should accept it."

Custer smiled and responded; "General" he said, nodding at Terry, "and Colonel", he added, looking at Colonel Gibbon. "That is truly a very generous offer and I thank you for it. I cannot accept it however. The 7th is a very close- knit unit. I have trained it to operate 'as one.' Adding four companies from another regiment would possibly break up the cohesion in the 7th that I have worked so hard to create. Also I cannot imagine encountering any force of hostiles that on its own the 7th, could not defeat. As such I must gracefully decline."

"Are you sure, Custer", Terry asked. "I could order you to take them you know."

"I understand that, General," Custer answered. "If you order me to take them I will of course follow your orders and do so. But I believe that these additional forces, not being part of the 7th, will slow us down and will not be necessary. The 7th, if it has to, can whip any group of hostiles on the Plains. And if by some chance the hostiles were able to defeat me, those additional four companies would not save the 7th." There is no doubt in my mind as to the truth of that, sir."

"All right, Custer, I will respect your decision," Terry answered. "On to another matter now. Do you want to take the Gatling Guns with you?" [6]

Custer responded, "General, I will decline those as well. As we all know, they are easy to overturn and the 7th will be moving through some rough terrain. They will only slow me down and I cannot conceive of a situation where we would need them. I have to move fast to ensure the hostiles don't escape us, and I can't be slowed down by dragging those weapons after me."

Terry looked seriously at Custer. "I will respect your decisions here, Armstrong. But I warn you. You had better be right and I truly hope you don't regret them."

The meeting broke up shortly after that and, after Custer left, Colonel Gibbon spoke privately to General Terry.

"General, I don't mean to question your judgment, but do you really believe it is wise sending Custer out there on his own? I don't believe he will wait for us. I believe that if gets the chance to attack the hostiles first, he will do so. And if the scouts are correct about the number of hostiles out there, I am not sure he and the 7th can handle

---

[6] Gatling Guns, were large, bulky rapid firing, horse drawn "cannons" that had multiple barrels. A soldier would stand at the rear side of the weapon, turning a crank, which would rotate the barrels, unleashing a heavy barrage of shells. These weapons were an early version of the 20th century machine gun.

them all."

"Colonel, I understand your fears in so far as Custer not waiting. History shows that if George Custer has an opportunity to attack he will do so. But he did demonstrate three years ago on the Yellowstone that he can be prudent when he fights and not be brash or reckless. He also didn't provoke a war with the Sioux when he went into the Black Hills two years ago. So, while he will seek an opportunity to attack, I don't believe that he will be reckless about it. And keep in mind that the President and Congress want to teach the hostiles a lesson. As such there is nobody better to do that than Custer. I can't think of anyone else better suited to track them down and force them into a bloody fight, and I have no doubt he can whip them. I don't care how many Indians are out there. They cannot defeat a unit like the 7th. And to be honest, Colonel, he has earned this opportunity. The President was really hard on him. He needs a shot at redemption and I am giving him that opportunity."

Colonel Gibbon snapped a sharp salute at Terry and responded; "I understand, sir."

As this conversation was occurring, George Custer hustled back to his unit. His heart was racing. General Terry was giving him a chance to save his career! He was going to be able to "cut loose" from Terry and pursue the Indians on his own. He was going back into his element – the "wolf tracking its prey!" When he got to the 7th's encampment, he ordered the bugler to sound "Officers Call." When his officers were surrounding him, Custer began to speak.

"Gentlemen, I am pleased to announce that the 7th is moving out on its own tomorrow. General Terry is giving us the responsibility of following the trail and ensuring the hostiles don't escape. It is the belief of General Terry that the 7th is the best unit to carry out this mission. I for one agree, and I know you all do as well."

At that last sentence there was spread cheers and smiles amongst the officers. They all knew without a doubt that there was no better cavalry unit the world than the 7th Cavalry, and that George Armstrong Custer was the best cavalry officer there was.

Custer smiled at the response. "The scouts feel that the hostiles are in the Valley of the Little Big Horn. We are to rendezvous with General Terry and Colonel Gibbon in that area on June 26. Our mission, again, is to prevent the hostiles from escaping before General Terry's column can reach there."

He paused and then went on, "I want you all to know that Colonel Gibbon offered us four of his cavalry companies. I told him the 7th was the best unit there is and that we didn't need them. I also declined the Gatling Guns as they will only slow us down."

At that, Captain Frederick Benteen spoke up. Never a fan of Custer, he made it clear that he didn't share Custer's opinion regarding the additional troops.

"General", he began, nodding at Custer. "While I agree that the 7th is the finest cavalry unit there is, I for one feel we should accept those additional troops from Colonel Gibbon. We all concur that we are pursuing perhaps the largest group of hostiles ever encountered. Those additional troops may prove to be very helpful to us. General, with all due respect I think you should reconsider this. As for the Gatling Guns, I agree with you. Their firepower would be nice to have; however, they are too cumbersome and will slow us down."

Custer bristled at Benteen's first comment. "Captain Benteen, your opinion is duly noted. I will stick to my decision, however, as I have no doubt that the 7th can accomplish this mission on its own. We won't be sharing this victory with any other units. This upcoming victory will belong to the 7th and to the 7th alone."

Custer then changed the subject and, speaking in his usual brusque manner, said, "I want all company commanders to ensure that their men are prepared and equipped to spend 15 days in the field. This means, that each man will carry enough forage for their mounts for 15 days. As well, each trooper will carry 100 rounds of carbine ammunition, and 24 rounds of pistol ammunition. At the beginning of each morning march, every company commander will report directly to me when their companies are fully prepared to move out. The last company to report readiness will remain behind the main column guarding the pack train. As well I want to be clear. Fifteen days is an estimate. If we haven't found them in 15 days we are not stopping or turning back. We only stop after we find the hostiles. So I'd advise all of you to tell your men to pack a lot of salt. We may be reduced to eating horsemeat and the salt will help with that. I want to be clear about something else. There are to be no bugle calls without a direct order from myself, and myself only. We are going to operate as quietly as possible.

Are there any questions gentleman?" Custer asked, wrapping up the meeting. There were some general questions posed to him that he quickly dispensed with. After that, the meeting broke up and the officers hurried back to their own companies to inform their troops of what was upcoming.

The next morning, Captain E.W. Smith of the 18th Infantry, which was part of Colonel Gibbon's command, came to Custer's tent with written orders from General Terry. The orders read:

Headquarters of the Department of Dakota (In the Field)

Camp at Mouth of Rosebud River, Montana Territory
June 22nd, 1876

Lieutenant-Colonel Custer,
7th Calvary

Colonel: The Brigadier-General Commanding directs that, as soon as your regiment can be made ready for the march, you will proceed up the Rosebud in pursuit of the Indians whose trail was discovered by Major Reno a few days since. It is, impossible to give you any definite instructions in regard to this movement, and were it not impossible to do so the Department Commander places too much confidence in your zeal, energy, and ability to wish to impose upon you precise orders which might hamper your action when nearly in contact with the enemy. He will, however, indicate to you his own views of what your action should be, and he desires that you should conform to them unless you shall see sufficient reason for departing from them. He thinks that you should proceed up the Rosebud until you ascertain definitely the direction in which the trail above spoken of leads. Should it be found (as it appears almost certain that it will be found) to turn towards the Little Bighorn, he thinks that you should still proceed southward, perhaps as far as the headwaters of the Tongue, and then turn toward the Little Horn, feeling constantly, however, to your left, so as to preclude the escape of the Indians passing around your left flank.

The column of Colonel Gibbon is now in motion for the mouth of the Big Horn. As soon as it reaches that point will cross the Yellowstone and move up at least as far as the forks of the Big and Little Horns. Of course its future movements must be controlled by circumstances as they arise, but it is hoped that the Indians, if upon the Little Horn, may be so nearly enclosed by the two columns that their escape will be impossible. The Department Commander desires that on your way up the Rosebud you should thoroughly examine the upper part of Tullock's Creek, and that you should endeavor to send a scout through to Colonel Gibbon's command.

The supply-steamer will be pushed up the Big Horn as far as the forks of the river is found to be navigable for that distance, and the Department Commander, who will accompany the column of Colonel Gibbon, desires you to report to him there not later than

INTO THE VALLEY OF DEATH

the expiration of the time for which your troops are rationed, unless in the mean time you receive further orders.

Very respectfully, Your obedient servant,
E. W. Smith, Captain, 18th Infantry A. A. J. G.

When Custer read the line "unless you shall see sufficient reason to depart from them" he grinned. This was exactly what he wanted. He had his orders but within them there was enough "leeway" to allow him to use his judgment and strike first at the enemy. The "finest pure predator" on the western frontier was being turned loose and he could not be happier!

At noon that day, Custer had his mighty 7th Cavalry Regiment assembled in front of General Terry and Colonel Gibbon. Terry and Gibbon reviewed the troops and Custer began to move out. As they began to march, Gibbon called out to him; "Now Custer, don't be greedy. Wait for us!"

To which Custer said with a laugh; "No I won't." With that, the "Boy General" put his spurs to his mount and took off at a gallop at the head of his men.

CHAPTER VII
TO THE VALLEY OF DEATH

The 7th Cavalry, along with a group of Crow and Arikara scouts, now began its march to what many felt back in May as it left Fort Abraham Lincoln was its rendezvous with destiny. George Custer - the greatest predator of the frontier was again tracking his prey. He wouldn't stop until he caught it.

That day, the regiment, after leaving the column of Terry and Gibbon, rode hard until approximately 8:pm when Custer ordered a halt. The officers and soldiers immediately dismounted and began to care for their horses. A good cavalry soldier knew that his life may depend having a healthy mount so he always made sure his horse was fed and otherwise taken care of before he took care of his own comforts. Once the horses were properly cared for, cooking fires were started, coffee was brewed, and most troopers settled down to a dinner of boiled coffee and hardtack.

After dinner, canteens and bottles full of whiskey appeared and for the first time all day the soldiers of the 7th Cavalry were able to relax. The officers could not relax yet however. Custer ordered "Officers Call" and they gathered at his tent. What occurred next surprised all who were present. Custer, who rarely, if ever, explained why he made the decisions that he did, opened up to his officers in a way never seen before.

"I will be glad to listen to any suggestions from any officer of the command", he said, "if made in proper manner. But I want it distinctly understood that I shall allow no grumbling, and shall exact the strictest compliance with orders from everybody – not only mine, but with any order given by an officer to his subordinate. I don't want it said of this regiment as a neighboring department commander said of another cavalry regiment that 'It would be a good one if he could get rid of the old captains and let the lieutenants command the companies."

Captain Benteen appeared very annoyed at the remark over "grumbling" and questioned Custer as to if that remark was directed at himself. Custer's response was "I want the saddle to go where it fits."

Benteen flushed at that last remark He responded "General, let's be clear here. Have you heard of any grumbling or criticism from myself?"

Custer glanced over at his visibly upset Captain. "No, I never have" he said in a quiet tone of voice, and then added, "None of my remarks tonight were directed at yourself."

That left many of the officers curious as to whom they were then directed at. The only other possibility may have been Major Reno, who clearly was disliked by Custer.

After "Officers' Call" ended and the officers dispersed, Lieutenants Edward Godfrey, Donald McIntosh, Francis Gibson, and George Wallace walked together to their tents. They all remarked at how quiet and sensitive Custer had seemed – there was none of the brusqueness displayed that was usually so present with him. Lieutenant Wallace then turned to his friend Lieutenant Godfrey and said, "Godfrey I believe General Custer is going to be killed."

Godfrey looked aghast at the comment and responded, "Why Wallace, what makes you think so?"

"Because I have never heard Custer talk in that way before", he answered.

The remark from Wallace left the others in a deep, thoughtful silence. They returned to their own companies and joined their men in having a bite to eat and relaxing with a few shots of whiskey. After downing the whiskey, it was into the bedrolls for a few hours of fitful sleep before reveille sounded.

While the soldiers tried to sleep, Custer sat in his tent writing letters to Libbie and working on various military reports/dispatches via candlelight. Since his Civil War days he had been known for his extraordinary energy level. (His soldiers referred to him as "Iron Butt" or "Hard Ass" for his ability to ride for hours.) Custer could ride for 18 hours a day, spend two-three hours writing reports and letters, sleep for two hours and be up, fully refreshed and ready to go. This campaign was no different.

Friday, June 23rd the regiment was on the move before first light and thundering across the plains. That day and the next Custer and his regiment rode hard. This was vintage Custer – riding close to 12 hours or more per day. When he finally did allow a halt, his men and their mounts were almost dropping in exhaustion while he still had waves of nervous energy left.

As the 7th closed in on the hostiles, all around them there were signs of very recent Indian occupation of the territory they were passing through. At one point they came across a single intact Indian lodge. When the scouts cautiously entered it they found the body of a Sioux warrior who had recently died. (It would later be learned that the warrior had been killed the previous week in the Battle of the Rosebud.) The troopers also came across a Sioux burial scaffold. In both cases, the burial sites were grossly violated by Custer and his men. Artifacts were stripped from the sites, and the bodies thrown into nearby rivers. (One of Custer's scouts, Isaiah Dorman, was alleged to use flesh from one of the bodies as bait when he went fishing.) Most of the Crow and Arikara scouts were aghast at the desecration of the burial sites. They were sure the Sioux would avenge these actions in terrible fashion.

On Saturday, June 24th, Custer finally called for a halt around 8:pm. As the exhausted soldiers dismounted, they received word to keep their horses saddled and under no circumstances were they to light any cooking fires. Many of the veterans gave each other a knowing look. A night march was coming up by the sound of it, they all agreed.

Just after nightfall, the Crow scouts, who were commanded by Lieutenant Charles Varnum, rode into the 7th's bivouac. They informed Custer that the Indians' trail further ahead veered to the west along a tributary of the Rosebud River, towards the Little Big Horn. The trail itself was full of fresh pony droppings indicating that the trail itself was very new.

When Custer heard that, he turned to his brother Tom and said; "Tom, you do know what that means don't you?"

Tom replied; "Autie, it means they are along the Little Big Horn, just as we thought they are, and that we are gaining on them."

"It means they are along the Lower Little Big Horn, not the Upper", Custer responded. "The scouts have already told me that we are less than a day's march from the Lower Little Big Horn. Tom, we are so close now. They are not going to get away from us."

With that Custer told Tom to pass the word amongst the officers that they were to immediately report to him. Just as they gathered, a strong gust of wind from the south blew in and whipped across

Custer's personal red-and-blue headquarters flag, blowing it to the ground. Lieutenant Godfrey, muttering "what the hell," stuck it back into the dry, sun-hardened soil. Another blast of wind came in and once again the flag dropped. This time, Godfrey packed sagebrush around the staff of the flag to make it hold. When he finished, he looked at his fellow officers and commented, "I do hope that isn't a harbinger of things to come."

Custer glanced over at Godfrey and quietly said, 'I wouldn't worry too much about that."

When the officers were gathered, Custer explained what the scouts had discovered and then outlined his plan;

"We'll let the men and their mounts rest for another hour or so. At 11:pm I want everyone ready to move out. We are going to follow this trail until daylight and then ascertain exactly where the village is. When we know that, we are going let the men and horses rest for the day. I know everyone is exhausted. We'll move the command forward after sunset and surround the village. We'll attack at dawn on the 26th."

Captain Tom Custer then spoke up; "That is exactly what we did at Washita."

Custer, responding to his brother, said: "That is exactly right, Tom, and that is why we are doing it. It worked perfectly then and it will work now."

Captain Frederick Benteen, frown on his face spoke up. "General, what about General Terry and Colonel Gibbon? I may be incorrect here, sir, but my understanding is we were going to attack the hostiles along with their forces."

Custer, visibly annoyed with Benteen, answered in his traditional brusque manner, "Captain, if you recall what I said before we departed from General Terry, we expect to link up with him on the 26th. So we will be attacking, in all likelihood, with them. I do hope that I have addressed your concern," he finished with a sarcastic bite to his voice.

Benteen looked at his commanding officer and responded, "Yes, sir, you have."

With that Custer reminded his officers to have their troops ready to move out at 11:pm and ended the meeting.

The exhausted men and horses of the 7th were ready to move out as per Custer's orders at 11pm. Custer took the lead, along with the scouts, and through the inky darkness the regiment moved on. As they moved through the pitch black, all Custer could think of was that the hostiles may escape him. That, if it occurred, would be utterly catastrophic for his career. He had to catch them and strike before they knew he was near.

For the next three hours, the 7th Cavalry Regiment moved through the darkness. There was no moon that night and as such it was difficult for the regiment to stay together. Lieutenant Godfrey later commented on how he used the choking dust cloud kicked up by the horses as a navigational aid. As long as he remained within the cloud, he knew that he was still with his unit. Finally, around 2:am on Sunday, June 25,th Lieutenant Cooke, who was riding alongside Custer, turned to him and said, "General,", the quiet, sensitive Canadian began, "may I respectfully suggest we halt here? I am receiving word that some of the horses are so exhausted that they are falling behind and many of the men are falling asleep they are so tired. Captain Yates just told me one of his troopers fell asleep and then toppled out of his saddle. Sir, if we don't stop we are going to lose some men and horses and we cannot afford that."

Tom Custer was riding alongside his brother and he added, "Autie,

Cookie is right here. Not everyone is like you and can go with no sleep. And even if the men can, their mounts cannot."

Custer knew Cooke and Tom were correct. "All right", he said. "We'll halt here. Pass the word to stop and get some rest. Be ready to move soon after daylight though. We are close and I am not going to risk the hostiles getting away from me."

Once the word got passed, the soldiers literally fell out of their saddles from sheer exhaustion. Some took the time to wrap a blanket around themselves; others simply curled up on the ground and immediately fell asleep. Custer himself lay on the ground beside his mount, pulled his hat over his eyes, and fell into a fitful sleep.

CHAPTER VIII
INTO THE VALLEY OF DEATH

Just after daylight on Sunday, June 25 Lieutenant Charles Varnum, commander of the scouts, peered through his binoculars at what his scouts were claiming was a truly immense village and pony herd. Varnum, his eyes red with lack of sleep and dust, turned to scout Mitch Bouyer and insisted he couldn't see anything. Bouyer, who was half Sioux and half French-Canadian, had told him when looking for the pony herd, to look for "worms on the grass." Bouyer angrily said "Sir, the biggest village I have ever seen is down there."

Varnum, frustrated, still couldn't see a pony herd or village. Trusting his scouts completely though he sent two Arikara scouts back to the column to alert Custer.

When Custer was awakened by the scouts with the news of what they had found, he leapt on his horse and galloped to where Varnum was. Like Varnum, he was unable to see the village and pony herd. "I don't see anything," he grumbled as he peered through his binoculars. However, Custer also trusted his scouts, and knew that many times Indian scouts were able to see things that a white man could not. Deciding that they were correct, he headed back to the 7th's bivouac. When he got there, he received some stunning and very unwelcome news from Tom Custer.

"Autie", Tom began when his brother rode back into the campsite. "During last night's march, some boxes of hard tack fell off one of the mules in the pack train. Captain Yates send a squad back along the trail to find it, and they ran into some Indian children going through the boxes. Yates' men killed one of the children but the others escaped. Autie, we have been discovered."

George Custer felt his heart sink. He knew what would occur now. Those kids would go back to their village and tell everyone there that soldiers were nearby. The village would pack up and run. Custer would then be blamed for allowing the Indians to escape. This was an impending disaster that could only be dealt with in one way – an immediate attack by the regiment on the village. (Custer had no way at all of knowing that the escaping children did not belong to the main village – his target. They belonged to an outlining village and as such did not alert the main village as to the presence of soldiers.) He turned to Sergeant Michael Kenney of Company F and bellowed, "Sergeant, tell the trumpeter to sound "Officers Call."" Kenney, momentarily surprised at the sudden lifting of the ban on bugle calls, immediately recovered and gave the order to Chief Trumpeter Henry Voss. Voss began blowing "Officers Call," summoning the officers of the regiment to Custer. When the officers gathered, Custer quickly went through what Tom had told him and explained,

"There is only one thing we can do now. We are going to attack today, before the village can escape."

Major Reno spoke up, "Sir, I understand the urgency of situation we find ourselves in now. However the men are exhausted and even more importantly so are the horses. I am not sure they are really capable of action today."

Custer glared at his second in command."Major, I don't believe we have a choice. Or would you like to explain to Generals Terry and Sheridan that we were all too tired and that is why we let the hostiles escape?"

Reno, averted his eyes from those of Custer and quietly answered, "No sir."

"All right then", Custer exclaimed. He turned to Captain Thomas McDougall, commander of Company B. "Captain McDougall, your company will remain in the rear with the pack train. All other commanders will assign four men to your command. That pack train is too valuable to leave lightly guarded. We are moving out in 30 minutes. Get your men ready."

Scout Mitch Bouyer rode up to Custer and said "General, there are more Indians in that village then this regiment on its own can fight. If you go in there, you and your men will die."

Custer glanced at his scout, flashed a nervous smile and said 'Oh I think we'll get through them in one day okay."

Thirty minutes later, the 7th was on the move. Company B, as per Custer's orders remained in the rear with the pack train, while the remaining 11 companies formed the vanguard for the attack.

The next couple of hours were spent with the 7th pounding along the Indians' trail. Custer, as always, was pushing his men hard. At just about mid-day he called a halt and ordered Captain Benteen forward.

"Captain, Custer began. "You will take companies H, D, and K, and proceed on a left oblique scouting the first valley you enter. If you find nothing in that valley, proceed to the next one. Along with your scouting mission, you will block the escape of any hostiles that retreat in your direction once the attack begins."

Benteen, concerned about the size of the hostile village they were going to encounter responded, "General if the village is as large as the scouts say it is, and shouldn't we keep the regiment together?"

Custer, angry at having his orders questioned by the always prickly Benteen, simply glared at the Captain and said, "Carry out your orders, Captain."

Not about to let his point go, Benteen responded, "I am not sure I fully understand my orders, General. How many valleys do you want me to scout?"

Custer, about to explode, now snarled, "Damn it, Benteen! I said scout the valleys you come to and I mean scout them. How can you not understand that?"

Benteen, figuring he had pushed his luck enough with Custer, sullenly saluted and answered "Yes, sir." Following his lead, companies H, D, and K made up of approximately 115 soldiers split off from the main column and moved on a westward course on their scouting mission. The remaining eight companies continued moving towards where the scouts had indicated they thought the village lay, with Company B staying to the rear with the pack train.

About two or so hours after sending Benteen and his three companies on their scouting mission, Custer called another halt. The predator inside him was telling him he was very close to his prey and he was eager to launch his assault. He turned to Major Reno, and gave him the orders that would begin the Battle of Little Big Horn.

"Major Reno, you will take command of companies A, G, and M along with the scouts. You will charge the village at as rapid a gait to which you deem to be prudent and I will support you with the remaining five companies that will be under my command. Do you have any questions about these orders?"

Major Reno responded, "No sir, your orders are very clear. We will carry them out."

Major Marcus Reno, signaled for companies A, G, and M to split off and move to their attack positions. As he did this Custer called the officers of companies C, E, F, I, and L together. Speaking quickly, he organized his battalion for the upcoming battle.

"Captain Yates," he said, referring to his old friend and commander of Company F. "You will take your company and E Company and will operate on the left flank." He nodded at E Company's commander, Lieutenant Algernon (Fresh) Smith. "Fresh, you will report directly to George." Smith responded with a crisp, "Yes, sir."

Custer then turned to I Company commander Captain Myles Keogh. "Captain Keogh, you will take command of your company and Companies C and L. You will operate on the right flank."

Then, quickly turning to his brother Tom, he said, "Tom, you will stay with me and the headquarters unit. Lieutenant Harrington (referring to Henry Harrington, C Company's second in command), you have command of C Company while Captain Custer is assigned to the headquarters unit."

Lieutenant Harrington snapped a crisp salute at Custer and said, "Yes sir. You won't be disappointed with my unit today."

Custer smiled briefly and responded, "Lieutenant, I have never been disappointed in your performance or that of your company."

Harrington answered, "Thank you sir."

With that Custer and his battalion of five companies with a total of 225 men, moved northeast along the bluffs, leaving Major Reno and his battalion to launch their assault. Reno and his force of approximately 145 soldiers and scouts moved directly towards the village. As they forded the Little Big Horn River, many of the soldiers had to fight their mounts that were desperate to drink from the river. Once he got his battalion across, Reno reached into his jacket and pulled out a bottle of whiskey and took a long pull on the bottle. He was frightened and was in extreme need of some "Dutch courage." With the warmth of the whiskey in him, he looked through his binoculars and ahead he could see rising turmoil in the village. That his men had been spotted he could tell. He turned to his bugler and yelled, "Trumpeter, sound the charge!"

With bugles blaring, and flags furiously flapping, Reno's battalion thundered across the flat plains towards the massive Sioux and Cheyenne village. Many of the troopers had their huge Colt 45 revolvers drawn and were firing then towards the village. As they approached the village, they expected to see sheer terror gripping the village and a great flight of people out of it. Instead, what they saw horrified them. Hundreds of enraged Sioux and Cheyenne warriors were charging them from the village, like hornets swarming out of their nests.

George Armstrong Custer would have charged right into the mass of warriors and, in all likelihood, settled the battle then and there. Marcus Reno however was no Custer. Fearing certain disaster if he continued the charge, he ordered his battalion to halt, and form a skirmish line. The men responded quickly, every fourth man taking the reigns of his horse and three others and retreated to a large batch of timber that lay to the rear of the battalion. The other men formed a skirmish line. Once the line was formed Reno gave the order to fire, and the Little Big Horn valley was echoing with the deep booming blasts of the soldiers' Springfield carbines. While Reno's men were certainly generating a tremendous amount of gunfire, due to the parsimonious U.S. government, soldiers were issued with less than 20 rounds per year for marksmanship practice. As a result, most of the soldiers couldn't hit the proverbial "broad side of a barn" with their weapons. The Springfield rounds were fired wildly, and few hit any of the attacking warriors. Many of the rounds smashed through teepees in the village and killed innocent women and children. Hunk Papa Chief Gall lost almost his entire family in the village due to the wild fire from Reno's men.

INTO THE VALLEY OF DEATH

As his men pumped rounds at the warriors, Reno looked frantically for the promised support from Custer. Looking to the east on the bluffs, he spotted Custer and his command. Custer appeared to be waving his hat, cheering Reno and his men on. There was no indication at all that he was about to attack and relieve some of the pressure off of Reno.

For almost 30 minutes, Reno's battalion fought on the skirmish line. Now casualties were beginning to mount, as Indian bullets and arrows began finding their mark among the troopers. Reno turned to his adjutant, Lieutenant Benjamin Hodgson and exclaimed "Benny, where in the hell is Custer? We are getting murdered down here."

Hodgson looked at Reno, who was taking a quick nip from his whiskey bottle. "Major, I have no idea. The last I saw of him was on the bluffs. But I think we should pull back to the timber where the horse-holders are sir. We are too exposed out here."

Reno, grasped at Hodgson's suggestion. "Lieutenant you are correct. We have to pull back." Reno then began yelling at the top of his lungs, "Pull back to the timber."

With that the soldiers on the skirmish line began to withdraw towards the timber where the horse-holders were seeking cover. As the soldiers retreated they remained crouched over and returned the Indian's fire as best they could until they reached the shelter of the trees.

For the next 60 minutes or so, a violent, bloody battle raged within the timber. Soldiers sought cover behind trees and blasted away with their Springfields. Already many were cursing their weapons. Just as Custer had foretold, as the carbines heated up, the copper cartridges expanded and jammed in the breech. Soldiers were left using their knives to dig the jammed cartridges out of their weapon. Warriors galloped on horseback all around the timber, firing bullets and arrows into the brush.

Captain Thomas French, commander of M Company, scrambled through the brush, and staying low to avoid the hostiles' fire, approached Major Reno. He was horrified to see Reno taking a large swig from his whiskey bottle.

"Major", Captain French began. "We cannot hold this position much longer. The men are expending ammunition at a furious rate and we are taking casualties. We don't have the men or ammunition to hold here. And sir, you need to put that away," he said, nodding at the exposed bottle. "We need you thinking clearly."

Reno looked at French, his eyes wild. "Damn you French, don't tell me what to do. Focus on taking care of your men and I'll be in command here. Now where the hell is Custer?"

"I don't know where the General is sir", Captain French responded. "But I do know the men need to know that you are in command and thinking clearly. Now please get rid of that bottle."

With that, Captain French hurried back to his company. "Reno is loosing it," he thought.

Meanwhile George Armstrong Custer was alive and well. After watching Reno launch his attack, and subsequently form his skirmish line, he called Tom over to him. "Tom, I should have had you lead the attack. Damn Reno anyway, he is a yellow coward. Any other officer in the regiment would have pushed on. Now what we are going to do is this. We are going to continue along the bluffs here. The scouts tell me if we do that, we will come to an area where we can get across the river and strike the village. Once we do that, that will pull the pressure off of Reno and he can continue his attack. We'll smash the village between us."

Tom Custer looked at his brother and responded, "Autie that will work as long as Reno does resume his attack after we hit them. I hope he has the guts to do so."

Back in the timber, Major Reno was indeed "losing it." After gulping another swallow of whiskey, he turned to his Arikara scout Bloody Knife. "Bloody Knife what should I do? I don't where Custer is."

Bloody Knife just started to respond when a Sioux bullet came screaming through the smoke and dust and exploded through his skull. Bloody Knife's skull literally seemed to vaporize with the impact of the slug. Reno's face and tunic were immediately drenched in Bloody Knife's blood and brains. At that point, he completely lost all composure. Reno immediately ordered his men to "mount." As they mounted, he then countermanded the order and had them dismount. He then changed his mind again, ordering them to mount and once more ordered them to dismount. Chaos and terror were spreading through his battalion.

During the pandemonium in the timber, Captain Myles Moylan, Commander of Company A, turned to Captain French, and declared, "Tom, Reno has totally lost it. We have to get the men under control or we'll all die here."

French agreed, "It's up to us to settle things down. But Myles, if Reno doesn't get control of himself I will shoot myself. I'll deal with the court martial later."

Moylan grimly responded, "I'll be happy to put a bullet into him as well. Now let's get things calmed down. We'll get the men mounted and get the hell out of here. Maybe we can leave Reno behind."

The two officers, working with their sergeants, were able to restore some semblance of order despite the incoming rounds and arrows. Thomas French, before mounting his own horse, scrambled over to Lieutenant Donald McIntosh, the young Canadian half-Iroquois who commanded Company G.

"Mac" French began. "Custer has left us, Reno is drunk, and has lost his mind. We have to get the hell out of here. We are going to pull out, retreat across the river and make a stand on the bluffs until either Custer or Benteen arrives. I need you and G Company to cover our withdrawal."

Donald McIntosh looked at Captain French somberly. In all likelihood he and his men had been given a death sentence. Orders were orders though. He looked French in the eyes and responded, "Yes sir. We'll do our best to hold them off you."

French wished the young officer good luck and ran back to his own horse. Just as he mounted Major Reno bellowed, "All those who wish to save themselves follow me." Reno then galloped away, back along the trail in which his men had so recently entered the valley, followed by a disorganized "mob" of troops.

Captains French and Moylan roundly cursed Reno for this. They had hoped to execute some form of organized withdrawal, with Lieutenant McIntosh and G Company operating as the rearguard. This wasn't an orderly military retreat now. It was an utter rout.

Reno's forces poured out of the timber and in absolute terror ran from the battle scene. In the timber, McIntosh lost control of Company G and saw them flee before he could organize them into an effective rearguard. As he mounted up to join his fleeing men, a Sioux arrow ripped through his back knocking him off his horse and killing him.

The warriors were initially caught off-guard by the soldiers' "whole scale retreat" but they quickly responded, riding alongside the fleeing troopers, pumping arrows and bullets into them, trying to knock them from their mounts. The soldiers responded by leaning low across the necks of their galloping horses, drawing their Colt .45 revolvers, and firing back at their pursuers. Numerous warriors and soldiers were blown off their mounts by bullets and arrows. When the soldiers reached the Little Big Horn River they spurred their frantic mounts forward. The terrified cavalry horses began swimming across the river with the riders clinging to them for dear life. Warriors dove into the river and pulled soldiers off their mounts, leading to life and death battles using knives, fists, and even teeth, under the swirling waters of the Little Big Horn River. No quarter or mercy was either expected or given by either side.

During the retreat across the river, Lieutenant Hodgson, already wounded himself, had his horse shot out from underneath him casting him, into the swirling water. As he floundered in the river, a retreating trooper saw the wounded officer and screamed "Sir, grab my stirrup" and thrust his stirrup towards Hodgson. The officer grabbed the stirrup and was towed across the river. When they reached the riverbank, Hodgson rose, only to take an arrow through his back, killing him instantly.

As Reno's decimated battalion fought their way across the river, Custer and his five companies continued towards their "jumping off point." Finally they had reached a bluff where the entire village was visible. Reno had attacked the opposite end of the village, and from this vantage point things looked quiet, but the size of the village was clearly immense. Custer turned to brother Tom and Lieutenant Cooke and said, "Oh my god, the village is as large as the scouts said it would be. I have never seen anything so big in my life."

Mitch Bouyer, who unlike the majority of the scouts remained with Custer's battalion, simply rolled his eyes when he heard that. He had told Custer what he would be encountering and now he was sure there was going to be a terrible price to be paid.

Thinking fast, Custer turned to Trumpeter Giovanni Martini and said; "Trumpeter, I want you ride back along the trail, find Captain Benteen and tell him to meet me here with the pack train. If it is safe to do so afterwards, return to me. Otherwise remain with Captain Benteen."

Martini saluted sharply and wheeled his horse around ready to make the ride. Knowing Martini who was a recent immigrant from Italy, and who didn't speak fluent English, Lieutenant Cooke stopped him.

"Hold it a minute, Trumpeter. I will write this out for you." Cooke then pulled a pad of paper and a pencil out of his jacket and scribbled;

> *"Benteen,*
> *Come on. Big village.*
> *Be quick. Bring packs.*
> *W.W. Cooke.*
> *P.S. Bring pacs. "*

With Cooke's note in hand, Martini spurred his horse hard and galloped off. As he did, he turned back and saw Custer looking out over the village and heard him yell, "Hooray boys, we have caught them napping. Let's finish up with them and we can return to our station!"

Martini rode hard towards where he thought Captain Benteen would be. He could hear heavy firing coming from where Reno had attacked, and Martini assumed that Reno had the Indians on the run. After a hard 45 minute ride, Martini spotted a cavalry column ahead of him. It was Captain Benteen.

Benteen had been cursing Custer throughout the afternoon. As far as he was concerned this scouting mission he was on was nothing more than a "wild goose chase." He even wondered if Custer was getting him out the way so he (Benteen) would not share any of the glory of the 7th's impending victory. Finally, after over two hours of fruitless riding through empty valleys, Benteen called off the scouting mission and turned his battalion back towards where he felt the regiment would be in action. He then spotted a lone rider coming hard towards him. Soon he recognized Trumpeter Martini. Martini and his horse were exhausted when they reached Benteen. Benteen quickly asked, "Where is Custer?"

Martini responded in a mix of garbled Italian and English. Benteen tersely then asked, "Where are the hostiles?"

Martini answered, "They are skedaddling," and then handed Benteen the note from Lieutenant Cooke.

Benteen shook his head. Clearly the regiment seemed to be in action, but where and what was going on? He then read the note. Looking exasperated, he handed it to D Company commander Captain Thomas Weir and said, "I don't have the packs. They are with Captain McDougall and he is about 30 minutes behind us."

Weir read the note and responded "Captain this sounds like the General wants us to get to him awfully fast. I don't think we should wait. The pack train will catch up with us."

Benteen, the more senior Captain of the two, glanced at Weir and said firmly, "No. If I am to be of any use to Custer, I'll need the packs. We will wait for them."

Once Martini had galloped off, Custer called a quick conference of his officers. "George", he said, speaking to George Yates, commander of Company F. "We have to get the pressure off of Reno. Take your squadron down the coulee here and charge the village. That will force most of the warriors to break off their attack on Reno. Get some hostages while you're down there as the responding warriors will hesitate to hit us hard if we have their women and children."

Captain Yates responded, "Don't worry, General. My boys will burn that village to the ground and bring back enough hostages so that no warrior will dare to come within a mile of us."

Custer replied "Excellent," and then he then turned to Captain Myles Keogh. "Captain Keogh, you and your squadron will remain up here and keep the path open for Benteen to join us. Once Benteen gets here with the packs, we will hit the village. Between us and Reno the hostiles won't have any idea of what hit them!"

Keogh confidently responded, "General, my men will keep a path open that is wide enough to run a train through. Have no fear about that."

Those members of Reno's battalion who escaped the timber and got across the river now began climbing the bluffs. Their best chance of survival was to gain and hold the high ground and wait for Custer and/or Benteen. At the top of the bluffs Reno, only now showing some appearance of command authority, began trying to organize his shattered men into some form of organized defense. Screaming, "Hurry, form skirmishers, move, move," Reno tried to get the troopers into some semblance of organized defense for the attack he knew would be forthcoming on their position. Captains Moylan and French, who had been among those who escaped, did the bulk of the work here though as Reno was visibly drunk and at times incoherent. Both Moylan and French passed the word through their junior officers and sergeants to dig defensive positions and brace for an attack.

Benteen by this point was on the move, finally being goaded by Captain Weir into action. They could all hear far-off gunfire, and it was clear that a battle was raging. Benteen's battalion rode towards the sound of the gunfire and finally emerged on a bluff looking down into the Little Big Horn Valley. The sight they saw was "bone chilling". It was Reno's men fleeing in disorganized terror. The regiment wasn't retreating – it was being cut to pieces!

INTO THE VALLEY OF DEATH

Captain Benteen could accurately be referred to as cantankerous when it came to his dealings with Custer, but nobody could call him a coward. Seeing his comrades in mortal danger, Benteen gave the order for his men to draw their weapons, the bugler to sound charge, and his battalion plunged down the bluff, to the rescue of Reno's forces.

With the appearance of Benteen's forces, the hostiles attacking Reno broke off their assault and pulled back. In their eyes they had no idea of how many troops were coming and they pulled back to be safe. Benteen's three companies rode into Reno's defensive position and Reno rushed towards Benteen exclaiming, "Benteen, thank god you are here. Where is Custer? Where is Custer?"

Benteen saw that the distraught, obviously drunk, and blood splattered Major was incapable of command at the moment. Benteen stated loudly "He is probably grazing his horses someplace safe after leaving you just as he left Major Elliott at the Washita." He then informally assumed command, bellowing orders to his men to share ammunition with Reno's troops, he ordered the digging of defensive positions, and sent word to Captain McDougall and the pack train to hurry forward.

As Benteen was doing this, Captain Weir left Company D to speak to Reno and Benteen. "Major, Captain", he began. "The General gave us written orders to join him. With all due respect, I believe we need to follow those orders. The hostiles have at least for now broken off their attack on this position and I witnessed them withdrawing to the other end of the valley. The General may be there, and he may need us. Major Reno, I fully understand that you have taken casualties and may not be able to proceed. But I assure you Company D, along with Companies H and K are fresh and willing to join the General – as per his orders. Sir." He ended with a very pronounced "Sir."

Reno glared back at Weir and responded, "Captain I am the senior officer here and I am countermanding the General's orders. You will remain here. Is that understood?"

Weir was furious however he had no choice and quickly nodded his assent. As he wheeled his mount around and began to ride back to Company D's position, a loud crash of gunfire suddenly sounded, emanating from the other end of the valley. Reno's question of "where is Custer" had been answered. It was clear he was now hotly engaged.

And indeed he was. Following Custer's orders, Captain George Yates led his squadron of Company F (known as the "Bandbox Troop" due to the tight control over discipline and appearance he exerted on it) and Lieutenant Algernon Smith's Company E (known as the "Gray Horse Troop" for obvious reasons) down what is known today as Medicine Tail Coulee. Mitch Bouyer had reported that the Little Big Horn River was shallow enough at the bottom of the coulee for the soldiers to cross and attack the village. Custer and the headquarters unit remained at the top of the bluffs with Captain Keogh's squadron.

As Yates's men descended the coulee and approached the river, a series of gunshots rang out. The Cheyenne end of the village was just across the river, and a group of warriors had camouflaged themselves in the trees along the river- bank. These warriors knew they had to slow the soldiers down to give time for their comrades fighting Reno to reach them. Immediately, troopers began dropping from their saddles as the Cheyenne bullets slammed into them. Unable to spot the warriors through the trees, many troopers blindly fired their revolvers into the foliage. At the same time, the big army horses were floundering in the soft mud that was along the river- bank. Many of the horses were slipping in the muck and were becoming impossible to control. Looking down, Tom Custer turned to his brother and said,

INTO THE VALLEY OF DEATH

"Autie, get them out of there. The horses can't get through that mud. They'll get butchered down there. We'll find another place where we can cross the river and get into the village."

Captain Yates, fighting his horse and ducking enemy fire, glanced up at the senior Custer who, agreeing with Tom, gave him the signal to withdraw back up the coulee. As Custer gave the signal to withdraw, Tom yelled to Captain Myles Keogh, "Myles, give George's boys down there some covering fire."

Instantly Keogh reacted, ordering Company I to dismount and then deploy along the ridge. On his order they began heavy firing into the tree line with their Springfield carbines where the Cheyenne were hidden, covering the withdrawal of Captain Yates's squadron, back up Medicine Tail Coulee. Company I's heavy fire successfully suppressed the enemy gunfire, and allowed the "bulk" Companies E and F to make their escape.

The two companies of Yates's squadron finished their withdrawal back up Medicine Tail Coulee and the fire from the Cheyenne warriors in the brush line slackened off. As Yates reached the bluffs, Mitch Bouyer motioned for Custer to look to the west. At Bouyers's warning, Custer snapped his binoculars to his eyes and saw a massive force of hostiles riding through the village towards him. There were clearly more than a thousand hostiles on the move towards him! Still Custer was aggressive and looking to attack the village despite the now massive odds against his force.

Calling Yates over to him, Custer barked, "Captain Yates, take the lead. We are going to ride to the north. Mitch here will let us know when we reach another spot where we can ford the river. We have drawn the pressure off of Reno now so he can resume his attack and that will make things easier for us."

Custer then turned to Lieutenant Cooke and ordered, "Cookie, go to

Keogh. Tell him to keep a route open for Benteen to reach us with the packs, and keep those hostiles off of us."

Cooke galloped over to Keogh and passed on Custer's orders. Keogh immediately began deploying his three companies to support Custer's instructions. He ordered Lieutenant James Calhoun to take Company L and set up on top of what would later be known as Calhoun Hill in skirmish line order. Company C, now commanded by Lieutenant Henry Harrington, due to Tom Custer riding with the headquarters unit, was split in two. Half the company would guard the horse holders of Companies C and L while the rest deployed about 100 yards to the southwest of Company L. Company I, under Keogh's direct command, would deploy a few hundred yards directly to the rear of Company L. Keogh's directions to all his officers were clear, "Benteen is on the way with the pack-train. We have to keep a route open for him to reach the General."

James Calhoun and his second in command, Lieutenant John Crittenden, formed Company L into skirmish line order while Lieutenant Henry Harrington did the same with Company C. Calhoun peered through his binoculars and could feel the sharp, cold pang of mortal fear in his heart. He estimated that close to 500 hostiles were approaching his position and coming fast! James Calhoun's thoughts momentarily turned back to the note he had written his brother-in-law George Custer five years earlier.

"If you ever need me, you will not find me wanting."

He was going to get the chance to back those words up now and he thought, "Well Jimmi, the odds here aren't good. Let's hope Benteen gets here quickly as we won't be able to hold them off for long."

 He turned to Crittenden and said, "Make sure the men know to hold their fire until I give the word." Crittenden hurried along the skirmish line, passing on Calhoun's order.

INTO THE VALLEY OF DEATH

The mounted warriors closed in and finally Calhoun bellowed "Fire, volley fire!" The Springfields of Company L unleashed a torrent of destructive firepower on the attacking hostiles. Calhoun then amended his order to "Fire at will." Company L was now pouring volley after volley of fire into the attacking warriors. Although outnumbering the soldiers by greater than 10-1 the devastating fire from the troopers stopped the hostiles "dead in their tracks." Numerous hostiles tumbled from their horses with army rounds blasting through their bodies. Others hit the ground hard when their horses were shot out from underneath them. Both Calhoun and Crittenden along with their sergeants hurried up and down the skirmish line encouraging their men to keep up their heavy rate of fire and adding to their companies' firepower by firing their own Colt .45 revolvers. The Sioux and Cheyenne responded in kind, firing bullets and arrows that tore into the army ranks decreasing the numbers of troopers on the skirmish line.

The situation was the same with Company C. Lieutenant Harrington stayed mounted as he directed a devastating barrage against the on-rushing hostiles. Harrington rode back and forth along his skirmish line barking orders and encouragement and almost daring the Indians to try to blow him off his horse. Harrington, however, could see the sheer numbers of hostiles he was facing and thought that it was only a matter of time before his unit was over-run unless he was allowed to withdraw or Captain Benteen reached them.

Very quickly into this action it became apparent that Custer's men were being outgunned. The soldiers equipped with single shot Springfield carbines could fire an average of seven rounds per minute. And that was an optimum number as many of the Springfields, as they heated up, began to jam. When that occurred, a soldier would frantically dig the jammed cartridge out of the breech using his knife. The strong point of the Springfield was its range and stopping power, which were superior to anything the hostiles were armed with. If a hostile was hit by a Springfield round, that hostile was "going down." Those strong points, however, were nullified by the jamming. Stopping power and superior range mean little if your weapon can't be fired.

Many of the hostiles, on the other hand, were using new Winchester, Spencer, and Henry repeating rifles they had received from traders. They could fire an average of 15 plus shots per minute – over the twice the amount of firepower the soldiers could put out. So not only were the soldiers badly outnumbered, they were left to fight against tremendous odds with inferior weapons and ammunition.

As Companies C and L were engaged, Captain Weir, back at Reno's position, hurried to Captain Benteen. Pointing to the direction where the gunfire was emanating from, Weir said, "Captain, the General is down there and could be in trouble. You can hear the battle. Sir, he sent us written orders to join him. Permission to take my company and go to the sound of the firing, sir."

Benteen brushed Weir off. "Permission is denied. We will remain here."

Thomas Weir was fiercely loyal to Custer, and couldn't believe that Custer's orders were being ignored when he so clearly needed assistance. Weir then, in direct contravention of Benteen's orders, decided on his own to try and reach Custer. He knew that Custer would support this decision and he would not face military discipline for disregarding the order or Reno and Benteen. Weir left the defensive position being established and began riding to the sound of the firing. His second- in- command, Lieutenant Winfield Edgerly, saw him leave. Edgerly, thinking Weir had permission, got Company D mounted, and the entire company rode out in support of Weir. The company reached a bluff now known as "Weir's Point." Captain Weir peered through his binoculars and turned to Edgerly and said "Lieutenant, I can't see anything. There is too much smoke and dust. But the General is down there and he needs us."

INTO THE VALLEY OF DEATH

Reno spotted Weir and Company D leaving the position. At first he was furious at Weir's disobedience, but recovering from that he ordered Lieutenant Luther Hare to join Weir and order him to attempt to make contact with Custer. Hare galloped off to join Weir and pass on Reno's orders. As Hare rode off, Benteen ran over to Reno and asked, "Major where is Captain Weir and his company going?"

Reno drunkenly mumbled, "He is leaving to find Custer and so I ordered Lieutenant Hare to join him make contact with Custer, and inform him of our situation."

Benteen cursed, and responded, "Major I ordered Captain Weir to remain here. A single company has no chance of cutting their way through all those hostiles to find Custer. They will be annihilated. If you are not going to recall him then we need to mount up and join Captain Weir. "

Reno slurred, "Weir may just be able to find Custer. You don't know."

Without responding to Reno, Benteen stormed over to Captains French and Moylan, and ordered them to pass the word to the officers and enlisted men dug in on the hill to mount up. Myles Moylan was aghast at the order. "Benteen," he said. "We have badly wounded men here. Moving them could kill them."

Benteen gave Moylan a cold stare and responded: "Captain Moylan, there is a good chance those wounded and all of us will die regardless of what we do. Our best chance of survival may be to find Custer and reunite the regiment so we can take on these red bastards as a united command. Now, get ready to move out."

Captain Moylan simply saluted nodded his head and ran back to his company while Thomas French was spreading the word to the other officers and sergeants. The wounded were wrapped in horse blankets and carried by their comrades while the rest of the command mounted and followed after Captain Weir and Company D.

In a short period of time Major Reno and Captain Benteen joined Captain Weir on the bluff. Like Weir, neither Reno nor Benteen could make out anything in the smoke filled valley. Benteen snarled: "I can't see anything. There is no way we are taking this command down there and ride into who knows what. Captain Weir, post a guidon here and perhaps Custer will see it and bring his command to us."

Captain Weir grabbed one of Company D's guidons and rammed the post it was mounted on into the ground.

While Weir, Reno, and Benteen were peering into the smoke filled Little Big Horn Valley Custer was still on the offensive. He was galloping along the ridge line with Companies E and F poised like a cobra – ready to strike. Custer knew Benteen was on the way with the ammunition packs and that Keogh and his squadron had his rear covered. All he had to do now was to find another spot in the river shallow enough to cross, wait for Benteen to arrive with the packs (at which point Keogh's rearguard would have also withdrawn and joined Custer along with Benteen), and then his entire battalion could invade the village. The warriors would lose their will to fight once Custer had possession of the village and held hostages.

Companies C and L had now been fighting a successful battle for close to 40 minutes. Although badly outnumbered, and outgunned, they were miraculously accomplishing their mission of keeping a route to Custer open for Captain Benteen and the pack train.

Many of the Sioux and Cheyenne now tried a different tactic. Frustrated at the heavy firing from the soldiers and the resulting casualties, the warriors dismounted, put down their rifles, and switched to bows and arrows. A rifle is only effective as a "line of sight" weapon. A warrior had to expose himself, aim the rifle and fire at his target. With bows and arrows they could remain lying down, hidden in the tall grass and brush, and fire arrows in an arc towards the cavalry skirmish lines. You can't fire a bullet in an arc. An arrow however can be devastating. And they were. A rain of death began crashing down onto Companies C and L. First to panic were the horses and their holders. Arrows came out of the sky slamming into the horses. The horse-holders tried desperately to control their panicked mounts, but were unable to do so. The horses broke free and began to stampede out of the soldiers' position towards the Indians. Many of troopers panicked at the sight of their stampeding mounts. Their reserve ammunition was in the saddlebags on their horses. And their horses were their only escape route unless they wanted to walk hundreds of miles back home.

Hundreds more arrows followed. There was no defense to the projectiles coming in from the sky. Troopers were dropping like "flies", impaled by steel tipped Sioux and Cheyenne arrows. The rate of fire from the skirmish lines was dropping off dramatically. As the rate of fire from the troopers slackened, the dismounted warriors began creeping closer to their positions while continuing to fire arrows and the occasional gun shot.

Captain Myles Keogh watching the disaster being unveiled to the front of his dug-in I Company, made the decision to order Companies C and L to pull back to I Company's position. He turned to 1st Lieutenant James Porter, who was mounted beside him. "Lieutenant," Keogh began, "send messengers to Lieutenants Harrington and Calhoun and order them to withdraw back to this position."

Porter responded with "Yes, sir." He wheeled his horse around and rode to the Company I skirmish line. He pulled Private Joseph Broadhurst and Corporal George Morris away from the skirmish line and said, "Private Broadhurst, you are to ride to Lieutenant

Harrington and order him to fall back to this position. Corporal Morris, you are to ride to Lieutenant Calhoun and give him the same orders."

Both Broadhurst and Morris gave each other a grim look. The odds of getting through that maelstrom to the front of them and returning alive were not good. Nevertheless, they both mounted and rode towards their appointed positions. Neither got through. Private Joseph Broadhurst got to within 20 yards of Company C's skirmish line before being blasted from his horse with three arrows protruding from his chest. Corporal Morris was even less successful. Just 300 yards or so from the Company I position, an arrow arcing from the sky impaled his back, sending the lifeless soldier tumbling from his horse.

At the Company L skirmish line Lieutenant Calhoun watched his unit begin to disintegrate. He watched in horror as Lieutenant Crittenden dropped with arrows protruding from his neck and back. Looking frantically through his binoculars for some sign of Benteen, he could see through the smoke and dust, the guidon mounted by Captain Weir several miles away on the bluff. Calhoun in desperation screamed "Sergeant Butler."

First Sergeant James Butler scrambled over to Calhoun. Butler was caked with dirt, black gunpowder grime, and blood splatters but, luckily, as yet wasn't wounded. "Yes, sir," Butler responded when he got to Calhoun's side.

Pointing to where he could see the guidon flapping on the bluffs Calhoun ordered, "Sergeant, I want you to ride and bring back help. I don't know where the hell Benteen is, but we are getting cut to pieces here. We'll hold here as long as possible but bring back help."

Butler looked at his commanding officer and said, "I will do my best sir, or I will die trying." With that, Butler grabbed the reigns of one of the few remaining, unwounded horses and mounted up. He drove his spurs into the side of his mount and, screaming every profanity in his vocabulary, charged out of the soldiers' position right at the hostiles, while the remaining survivors of Company L gave him covering fire. The Indians were so amazed at the sight of the "crazy white man" riding right at them they actually let him through. Then realizing he may escape a group of them went after him.

First Sergeant James Butler was a superb horseman and he rode as if all the demons from hell were after him. His powerful horse pulled away from his pursuers and Butler could see off in the distance the guidon mounted by Captain Weir. Butler knew the presence of the guidon meant there were troops there. He had to reach them to give his comrades a chance at survival. The pursuing warriors fired at Butler but it seemed like a futile exercise until a round struck his mount. Butler's horse went down, sending the sergeant flying over the front of his mount and crashing heavily to the ground. Cursing, Butler grabbed his Springfield, lay behind the dead body of his horse and opened fire on the approaching hostiles. First Sergeant James Butler waged a one-man war for the next 10 minutes. He managed to kill three hostiles with his Springfield, until the red-hot weapon jammed. He then drew his Colt revolver and fought on with that. The remaining Sioux showered his position with arrows and bullets until the inevitable occurred. His body was found after the battle surrounded by over 25 spent cartridges. James Butler didn't "go quietly into the night."

Keogh, seeing no movement from either Companies C or L towards him and assuming his messengers had not gotten through to them, ordered Trumpeter John McGucker to sound "Retreat" in the hope that Calhoun and Harrington would hear that and begin a withdrawal. McGucker blew "Retreat" as loudly and powerfully as he could.

The end was near now for Companies C and L. Lieutenant Henry Harrington, who had been truly magnificent leading his small company, strained over the din of battle trying to hear what he thought was a bugle sounding retreat. Before he could ascertain exactly what he was hearing, he was blown off his horse by several arrows, killing him instantly. With their commanding officer dead, and their horses gone, panic took over. The survivors of C Company now broke ranks and ran fleeing towards Captain Keogh and I Company about a mile to the rear. With the troopers running, warriors jumped to their feet and charged in. Hundreds more leapt onto their horses and also charged. The fleeing troopers were slaughtered as they ran.

When the C Company position collapsed, Lieutenant Calhoun, trying to rally the survivors of L Company, saw a wave of hostiles swarming towards his position from where Company C had been. Calhoun screamed "To the right rear flank," trying to get some firepower directed at the hostiles approaching from there. A few troopers reacted as he directed and fired, while Calhoun blazed away with his now red- hot Colt revolver. It wasn't enough as Hunk Papa Chief Gall, enraged at the loss of his family in the Reno attack, led a mounted charge rolling over the remains of Company L. Lieutenant James Calhoun, keeping his word to Custer to the very end, died firing his Colt into the faces of Sioux warriors as they over-ran his position.

Custer was not aware of the impending disaster at his rear nor that Benteen wasn't coming. As he galloped along the ridge Mitch Bouyer, who was riding ahead of the battalion, suddenly halted. Custer ordered his column to halt as well and rode up to Bouyer along with Tom Custer. Bouyer grimly pointed to the north said "General, look at that."

Both Custers raised their binoculars and spotted what Bouyer had seen. It was a massive group of warriors led by Crazy Horse pouring out of the Oglala and Cheyenne areas of the village and moving to cut him off. George Armstrong Custer was an aggressive officer but

INTO THE VALLEY OF DEATH

he was no fool. He knew he couldn't take his two companies of slightly more than 80 men and ride through hundreds of warriors. He looked at Tom and said, "We can't get through there. We are fighting a defensive battle now, Tom. We have to get to the high ground and dig in and wait for Keogh and Benteen to join us. Then we'll strike back."

Tom Custer looked at his brother and remarked, "You are right, Autie. We can dig in and hold them off. When Myles and Benteen get back to us, then we'll whip them. It will just take a little longer than we originally thought," he added with a nervous smile.

Gall led a force of well over 600 warriors towards Company I. Myles Keogh, having seen the destruction of Companies C and L, had his Company deployed in proper skirmish line order. As Gall and his warriors charged in, Company I laid down a heavy defensive fire. Captain Keogh remained mounted, directing his men's fire at the on-rushing warriors. Again most of the warriors dismounted, as they had done with Companies C and L, and fired arrows in an arc down onto the soldiers. Others kept pumping their Winchester and Henry repeating rifles, pouring rounds into the soldiers' positions. As Keogh remaining mounted, directed the defense, a Winchester round tore through the side of his horse, blasting through his knee and sending him reeling off his mount. Private John Barry and Sergeant James Bustard rushed to his side.

"Sir, are you all right," asked the terrified Private Barry.

"Oh bloody hell, what hit me", Keogh muttered in his thick Irish brogue.

"Sir, we are going to get you out of here," Sergeant Bustard said.

First Sergeant Frank Varden scrambled over. "We have to get the captain under some cover," he said to Barry and Bustard, "while we keep these savages off of us."

Sergeants Bustard and Varden began pulling their wounded captain behind the skirmish line. It wasn't much protection but it was the best they could do at the time. Lieutenant Porter, I Company's second--in command ran in a crouch over to where Keogh was laid down. "Sir," Porter began. "Do you have any orders for me?"

Keogh, his face distorted from the excruciating pain he was feeling from his shattered knee, grabbed Porter's arm tightly, and responded, "Hold the line, Lieutenant. Benteen is on the way and we have to keep a path open for him to get to the General."

Porter answered, "Yes, sir" and then turned to return to the skirmish line. As he did so, an arrow exploded through his heart, knocking the young Lieutenant to the ground, mortally wounded.

With their leaders down, casualties mounting, and Sergeants Bustard and Varden at Keogh's side and away from the skirmish line, panic then took over Company I. Troopers began abandoning the skirmish line and trying to reach their mounts to escape. Others, watching the collapse of the skirmish line, and terrified at the thought of being captured, shot themselves. Sergeant Varden, seeing his company collapsing, sprang away from Keogh's side and attempted to restore order amongst the chaos.

"Reform the skirmish line," he screamed. "Hold your positions or I'll shoot you myself."

Just as the last words left his mouth, a Cheyenne arrow buried itself in his neck. Varden dropped his Colt, and while choking on his own blood, staggered back towards Keogh and Bustard and fell across the wounded captain who was prone on the ground. As Company I went to pieces, the dismounted Indians leaped on their horses, charging through what was left of the soldier's position, chasing after the fleeing soldiers. Many of the warriors who rolled over Company I compared it to a buffalo hunt. They just ran down the soldiers and slaughtered them. Sergeant Bustard, kneeling beside the wounded Captain Keogh, flung away his Springfield carbine and emptied his Colt revolver into the wave of warriors rushing towards him. A Sioux warrior named Fierce Chicken charged him waving a war club, and Bustard threw his now empty revolver at his face, knocking him to the ground. The fiery Irish born sergeant screaming, "C'mon you black-souled son of a bitch," yanked his Bowie knife from its scabbard leaped upon the warrior who was struggling to rise and buried the blade deep into Fierce Chicken's neck almost decapitating him. Scarlet Face, another Sioux, charged from behind and smashed Bustard's skull with a mighty blow with a war club. A split second after Bustard was struck, Captain Keogh sitting up and firing his revolver put two rounds into Scarlet Face's head. Brain matter and blood exploded from Scarlet Face's shattered skull and he collapsed. Before he could fire any more shots, Keogh was hit by multiple bullets killing him instantly. The rest of Company I was wiped out and now over half of Custer's battalion ceased to exit.

As the hostiles "mopped up Company I, Sioux warrior Many Flies spotted Benteen's command and the guidon on Weir Point. Screaming, "soldiers, more soldiers," he pointed towards the bluff. Heeding the warning of Many Flies, a group of warriors numbering perhaps 400 began charging towards the troops on Weir Point. Benteen seeing this, ordered a retreat back to Reno's original position. With Benteen's withdrawal the majority of the warriors turned back and began racing to catch Custer's command.

Custer and his brother Tom, were in the midst of deciding where their battalion would dig in when Lieutenant Algernon Smith galloped up to them. Company E had been in the rear of Custer's march and they had spotted Gall's force that had finished off Keogh's battalion heading towards them.

"General," Smith began. "Sir, I have to report we have a large group of hostiles approaching us from the rear." He paused and then added, "Sir, the rear-guard must have fallen."

Custer for a moment looked ashen and lost. "My god, Myles, Jimmi, Henry gone?"

Mitch Bouyer now yelled, "General, whatever you are going to do, do it now." He pointed to Crazy Horse's forces charging in from the north, and now Custer also had to deal with Gall coming at his rear.

Snapping out of it, Custer pointed to a small hill on his right. He yelled, "Let's get to that hill men. Move, move!"

As his battalion stormed up the hill, Custer bellowed, "Captain Yates, Lieutenant Smith, dismount your men. Dismount your men. Form skirmish lines!"

The two companies, along with the headquarters unit, dismounted. The skirmish lines formed up while the horse-holders looked frantically for some area of safety.

Most of the warriors dismounted. They hid in the deep grass and brush as they crept and fired towards the soldiers. Arrows and bullets were slamming into the soldiers, who responded with volleys of fire from their Springfields. George Custer was using his Remington sporting rifle to deadly effect. Always a lethal marksman, he dispatched several warriors "to the great beyond" with a well aimed shot. Beside him, Tom Custer worked the lever on his personal Winchester repeating rifle, adding to the heavy defensive fire. Lieutenant Cooke, loyal as always, remained at Custer's side, firing his Henry repeating rifle. To bolster the defense, Custer now ordered, "Shoot all wounded horses and pile them up as breastworks. Men, we have to hold on!"

The wounded horses were quickly shot, and their bulk provided a level of protection.

INTO THE VALLEY OF DEATH

Tom Custer turned to his brother and said, "Autie, we have to drive those bastards back or they will overrun us before Benteen can get here. Get Fresh and his boys to push them down the hill. That will buy us some time."

Realizing Tom was correct, and that he could not allow the hostiles to get any closer, Custer turned to Cooke and said, "Cookie, tell Fresh to take his company on foot and charge the right flank of the hostiles. Drive them back. Once they do they are to withdraw back here. That will give us some breathing space."

Cooke scrambled over to where Lieutenant Algernon "Fresh" Smith and Company E was deployed. "Lieutenant, the General wants you to take your company and charge the hostiles on the right flank on foot. If you can push them back, it will buy some time for Benteen to reach us. Once you push them back, withdraw back to here."

Smith looked at Cooke and responded, "Okay, Cookie. We'll do our best." Smith then called First Sergeant Frederick Hohmeyer over. Smith outlined the orders and told Hohmeyer to "Have the men ready to move on my orders."

Hohmeyer quickly spread the word, and minutes later, led by Lieutenant Smith, Company E stormed out of the barricaded position and charged the threatening hostiles. Company F poured covering fire into the enemy position to cover the charge. Initially caught off guard, the Indians fell back in utter disorder. That didn't last long, as the Sioux and Cheyenne quickly saw how small Smith's attacking force was. They counter attacked, hurling Company E back.

As the soldiers fell back under heavy fire, military discipline began to break down. Twenty- eight men, or more than half the company, launched a desperate attempt to escape rushing into what is now known as "Deep Ravine." It turned out to be a death trap. The walls of the ravine were steep, and when the soldiers charged in they quickly saw they couldn't get out. Indians from above poured fire down on them, and then jumped in, finishing off any wounded survivors. In the wild frenzied action in the ravine, Private John Henderson, yet another young Irish immigrant who had sought a better life in the United States, crushed the skull of one Sioux with the butt of his Springfield and then was tackled by a Cheyenne named Running Rabbit. Henderson and Running Rabbit grappled on the ground until Henderson was able to draw his Bowie knife and rammed the blade right through Running Rabbit's left eye, deep into his brain, killing him instantly. A moment later White Antelope, Running Rabbit's cousin smashed in Henderson's skull with a tremendous blow from a stone war club.

Lieutenant Smith was one of few members of Company E not to get caught in "Deep Ravine". Wounded in the leg, he struggled to get back up the hill and the 7th's last defensive position. As he labored to get up the hill, two Cheyenne warriors rushed him from behind. Lieutenant Cooke, peering over the side of a dead horse, spotted Smith's situation and screamed, "Fresh, get down." At his friend's warning, Smith hit the ground, and Cooke rapidly blew both warriors away with his Henry rifle. Private Patrick Bruce of F Company witnessed Cooke's superb display of marksmanship and said, "Nice shooting Lieutenant. Lucky though you had that Henry, sir cause you couldn't shoot like that with this shitty Springfield."

Cooke nodded at Private Bruce just as Smith scrambled to his feet and made it to the dubious safety of the soldiers' position, diving over the barricade of dead horses when he arrived. Lieutenant Smith would live for a few more minutes anyway.

As the fighting raged, dozens of Sioux and Cheyenne women charged up the hill, braving the soldiers' heavy gunfire, waving blankets and screaming in an effort to frighten the cavalry horses. The blanket-waving, screaming women, added to the rain of arrows, had the desired effect. The terrified horses broke away from the desperate horse holders and stampeded away. Just as it was in the battle for "Calhoun Hill," the loss of the horses had a devastating impact on the encircled, trapped soldiers. Their reserve ammunition was now gone. And if Custer's men survived, they were going to have to walk home.

Tom Custer, while keeping up a heavy stream of fire from his Winchester, turned to his brother and yelled, a touch of hysteria now in his voice, "Autie, Benteen isn't coming, and I think Autie Jr. (Arthur Reed) and Boston are down. What the hell are we going to do?"

Custer firing his Remington, yelled at Tom "Benteen is a bastard but he is coming. He'd never let me down." His mind was working at a furious pace. There had to be a way out of this situation, he just knew it! Custer turned to Chief Trumpeter Henry Voss and bellowed "Trumpeter blow 'Assembly Call'. Blow, damn it, blow!"

Voss, in a desperate effort to attract Benteen's attention, blew "Assembly Call" with every bit of strength in his lungs. Surely, the few remaining soldiers thought, with the bugle blaring and guns booming, someone has to hear us and come to our aid.

Captain Yates crawled over to Custer and said, "General with the horses stampeded most of our reserve ammunition is gone. We can't ...

George Yates never spoke another word. A Sioux bullet removed most of the top portion of his skull and the captain collapsed against Custer. Custer shook the body of his old friend off of him and continued firing.

The barricade of dead horses offered some protection against rifle fire, but not arrows, and casualties were mounting. There were now less than 40 men left alive on Last Stand Hill. An arrow burying itself in his chest abruptly silenced Henry Voss. Custer saw Voss drop and, with his mind racing, tried to think of another strategy to save the remnants of his command. As he did this, he was peering through the sights of his Remington, finger on the trigger, when he received a hammer like blow in his left breast and flew backwards. Tom saw his brother go down and rushed to his side.

"Autie, oh my god, are you hurt?" the younger Custer cried out.

George Custer tried to rise, but the pain was excruciating. He coughed heavily, and blood sprayed from his mouth. During the Civil War he had always led his men into battle. He had over 10 horses shot out from underneath him and all that time only suffered one very minor wound. His luck had now clearly run out.

Mitch Bouyer, who had been fighting very effectively, saw Custer go down and now decided all was lost. He yelled out "The General is down. Let's get out of here. Follow me. We'll cut our way through, down to the river, and escape."

With that, whatever cohesion was left on the hill disintegrated. Bouyer jumped over the barricade of dead horses and, followed by 25 troopers, began a desperate run down the hill towards the Little Big Horn River. Tom Custer, outraged at the sight of his brother being abandoned, shot two of the fleeing troopers dead. He then turned back to his critically wounded brother as Bouyer and his party vanished into a maelstrom of enraged warriors.

"Autie", he said over the din of battle. I'm sorry. Bouyer and most of the men just bugged out on us. They won't get far though."

George Custer, his face contorted in agony, pulled one of his Webley pistols from its holster.

'Tom" he said with a raspy voice, blood streaming from his mouth, "get me up. Let me look those red devils in the face."

INTO THE VALLEY OF DEATH

Tom and Lieutenant Cooke struggled to help Custer get up when they saw death in all its majestic horror coming straight at them and those few remaining alive on Last Stand Hill. Crazy Horse saw Mitch Bouyer's party get wiped out and decided it was time to finish the battle. Screaming "Hokahey[7], it's a good day to die," Crazy Horse led a charge of close to 200 mounted warriors towards the barricade on top of Last Stand Hill.

Custer, with help, struggled to his feet and watched the mass of warriors closing in. With his last ounce of strength, he pulled the trigger on his Webley revolver, firing a single shot towards the onrushing horde and then collapsed. Tom knowing there were only seconds left, leaned down and drew his own Colt revolver. He placed it against his brother's left temple and said, "I won't let them get you Autie." He then pulled the trigger. He leaped to his feet and, while screaming "C'mon you red bastards," fired his Winchester repeatedly into the mass of charging warriors.

Led by Crazy Horse, the mounted warriors leaped over the barricade firing their own rifles, and swinging war clubs. There was one final, furious explosion of fighting on the hilltop. Sergeant Michael Kenney, having flung away his Springfield and fired all 24 rounds of pistol ammunition, yanked one Cheyenne from his horse and buried his Bowie knife into his neck. Sioux warrior Screaming Eagle tackled him and the two rolled on the ground throwing punches. At one point Kenney got the upper hand, pinning Screaming Eagle to the ground and bent down biting a massive chunk of flesh out of his cheek. The Sioux shrieked in agony. A moment later, Cheyenne warrior Poor Dog smashed in Kenney's skull with a tomahawk. Screaming Eagle, his face gushing blood from its horrific wound,

---

[7] The most exact translation would be "Let's do It."

snatched the tomahawk from Poor Dog and in an absolute frenzy pounded Kenney's skull and brains into jelly.

Cooke, was firing his Colt revolver when a Sioux warrior ran a lance through him from behind. Cooke looked dumbly at the lance tip with a huge chunk of his heart sticking to it protruding from his chest. He then collapsed. Tom was swinging his now empty Winchester as a club when a Cheyenne shot him through the head. Now the only living humans on the hill were Sioux and Cheyenne.

The Little Big Horn battle wasn't over yet. With Custer defeated, the warriors turned their attention back to Reno and Benteen, while Cheyenne and Sioux women moved around the Custer battlefields, killing any wounded soldiers who were still alive and stripping and mutilating the dead. Bodies were scalped, limbs and genitals cut off, eyes gauged out, etc. Remarkably, one body that was left "intact" was that of Captain Myles Keogh. He was stripped like all the dead, however he was not desecrated in anyway. The only possible reason for this was the St. Christopher medal hanging around his neck. Apparently, the Indian women felt that medal was "powerful medicine," and they didn't want to disturb the body.

For the remaining period of daylight, the Indians pumped heavy fire into the dug in troops on what is now known as Reno Hill. At nightfall, the Indians broke off their attack, leaving snipers to fire isolated shots into the troopers' position throughout the night. First Sergeant John Ryan of M Company, armed with a telescopic sighted Sharps buffalo hunting rifle, returned fire through the night, aiming at every enemy rifle flash that he saw. Ryan's return fire was so accurate that the Indians' sniper fire slackened off dramatically.

During the night the soldiers' position was filled with the cries of the wounded. Dr. Henry Porter worked throughout, desperately tending to the wounded who were in agony from pain and lack of water. Aware of their comrades' great suffering, several troopers, risking almost certain death, slipped out of their defensive position and down to the river returning with water for the wounded. Without a doubt these men were among the bravest ever in the long and glorious history of the United States Army.

Just before sunrise, the Sioux and Cheyenne resumed their attack on the Reno/Benteen position. Captain Benteen failed Custer greatly the day before, but on this day he was magnificent. Refusing to take cover, he walked upright amongst the troopers, barking orders and encouragement. He mocked and taunted the enemy, daring them to shoot at him. When a Springfield jammed, he grabbed it from the soldier, pried the cartridge out, and handed it back. Reno on the other hand huddled by himself doing little to lead his men.

The battle raged non-stop into the early afternoon. By this point, Indian scouts had become aware of the approach of the General Terry and Colonel Gibbon's column of troops. Now, many warriors argued for one final massive charge that would sweep over the soldiers' position and kill them all[8] . Sitting Bull counseled against that. He said, "If we kill all the soldiers, the wasichus[9] will never rest until they kill us. No, let these soldiers go and return home and tell their people of the power of the Sioux and Cheyenne. They will then leave us be."

Sitting Bull's advice was taken. The warriors gradually disengaged from their attack and the massive village along the Little Big Horn scattered. The Battle of Little Big Horn was over.

On Tuesday, June 27, 1876, General Terry's column marched into the valley of the Little Big Horn, and was met by forces sent by Major Reno. Terry's troops had already come across the Custer

---

[8]Such a strategy would have in all likelihood resulted in extremely heavy Indian casualties and the total destruction of the 7th Cavalry regiment.

[9] Wasichus was the Sioux term for white people

battlefield, and they broke the news to the Reno/Benteen battalion on what had happened to Custer.

For the men who had fought for two days and questioned, "Where is Custer?" the site where the five companies under him fought and died was horrific. Most of the soldier's bodies were terribly mutilated and bloated from the hot sun. Like the aftermath of the Fetterman battle, bodies were stripped and scalped, limbs and genitals chopped off, abdomens cut open, etc. Custer was found stripped naked with single bullet wounds in his left breast and left temple. He was not scalped. His ear drums had been punctured by sewing needles and a stick rammed up his penis. Outside of that his body was left alone. Tom Custer was so badly mutilated that he could only be identified by a tattoo on his arm. Looking at the horribly mutilated bodies, Lieutenant Godfrey who had survived along with Reno and Benteen, muttered, "How they must hate us."

As they walked along the battlefield, it was clear to officers such as Frederick Benteen and Colonel John Gibbon, that "Custer's Last Stand" had actually been a series of battles. There was the long, sustained, savage combat on "Calhoun Hill" and the surrounding area where Companies C and L fought so long and so bravely. Lieutenant Calhoun's body was found surrounded by a pile of empty Colt cartridges indicating he had personally put up a tremendous fight before being killed. There was the site where Company I seemed to have rapidly disintegrated, putting up minimal resistance. There was "Deep Ravine" where most of Company E died in a panic. And then there was "Last Stand Hill" where Company F, along with the headquarters unit, put up a dogged resistance until the end.

Captain Benteen was scathing in his view of the Custer battlefields. He called it a "rout," suggesting there was clear evidence of panic across the battlefield, with the exception of Companies C, L, and Last Stand Hill. To Benteen, this indicated a breakdown in military and command leadership. (As always he was a critic of Custer.)

Certainly in a sense, Benteen was not completely wrong. There was clear evidence of panic on the battlefield. That is very understandable when one remembers that white soldiers had been told from early on that to be captured alive by Indians was "a fate worse than death." Factor in these young soldiers watching their leaders and friends dying in front of them, their weapons jamming at times, and it is no wonder. That being said, with the evidence both from where the bodies of soldiers had been found and from testimony from the Indians themselves, Custer had made intelligent decisions on the deployment of his troops, properly deploying rear guards, advance guards, etc, and there were areas of sustained military resistance. The fact that they were not successful does not necessarily mean the entire command structure collapsed, as Benteen would want people to believe.

AFTERWORD

The Battle of Little Big Horn was the greatest military triumph ever for Native North Americans over conventional military forces. And yet in the end, it did nothing to preserve the Indians' way of life. As Sitting Bull had feared, when white Americans heard the news of the destruction of the 7th Cavalry Regiment, they demanded revenge. More troops were rushed to the western frontier and the Sioux and Cheyenne were pursued without mercy. Many of the Indians decided that resistance was futile and agreed to return or move to the reservations.

Sitting Bull convinced the Hunk Papa that their only hope of survival as a free people was to move to Canada. Canada always had a less bloody history of dealing with Indians than did the United States. (Many Indians, however, would find out that the Canadian government was as dishonorable as the U.S. Government. Canada simply persecuted their natives through the use of lawyers and one-sided treaties as opposed to military force.)

Beginning in November 1876, Hunk Papa Sioux began crossing into Saskatchewan. The Canadian government based in Ottawa, Ontario, was horrified. Canada had a very small army and was in no position to try to battle the same Sioux forces that had destroyed Custer. Superintendent James Walsh of the North West Mounted Police (now the Royal Canadian Mounted Police) was given the task of negotiating with Sitting Bull.

Superintendent Walsh took a small party of Mounted Police officers with him. He ensured that the "Mounties" as they had already been nicknamed wore their ceremonial red tunics as he wanted to ensure that they did not in anyway resemble American soldiers. He later wrote of the fear he felt riding into the Sioux camp, being surrounded by Indians wearing blood soaked 7th Cavalry uniforms and carrying army weapons captured at Little Big Horn. It appeared that there were more guns in Sitting Bull's camp in Saskatchewan then the entire Canadian army had in all of Western Canada! Sitting Bull and the Sioux for their part were flabbergasted that Walsh and his police officers would simply ride into their camp unannounced. They respected the courage of the Mounties no doubt but many questioned their sanity!

Walsh met with Sitting Bull, and told him that he and his people were welcome to stay in Canada provided that they caused no trouble and did not use Canada as a base for raids into the United States. He also indicated that Ottawa did not view the Hunk Papa as "Canadian Indians," therefore there would be no government assistance given to Sitting Bull and his people by the Canadian government.

Over the next four years, Superintendent James Walsh and Sitting Bull developed a close personal relationship. Canadian Prime Minister Sir John A Macdonald was extremely nervous having Sitting Bull in Canada and he wanted the Hunk Papa out. Great Britain, which was still responsible for Canada's foreign relations, also wanted Sitting Bull and the Hunk Papa out. The British were concerned that the United States would view the presence of Sitting Bull and his people in Canada as a provocation.

Under heavy pressure from Prime Minister MacDonald, Walsh arranged for a meeting between Sitting Bull, and General Alfred

INTO THE VALLEY OF DEATH

Terry at Fort Walsh, Saskatchewan in October 1877. (Walsh had commanded the building of the fort and named it after himself.) Sitting Bull had initially refused to meet with Terry but under pressure from Walsh had finally agreed. The meeting went nowhere. General Terry, while being a fine, educated gentleman, was simply viewed by Sitting Bull and the Hunk Papa as the man who sent Custer to his doom and a lackey of the United States Government. Terry returned to the United States having failed in his mission.

Still eager to get Sitting Bull and the Hunk Papa out of Canada, Prime Minister MacDonald arranged for Walsh to be transferred to Fort Qu'Appelle, Saskatchewan in 1880. MacDonald had decided that Walsh and Sitting Bull had become too close and their friendship would stand in the way of Sitting Bull and his people returning to the United States. (He was probably correct.) In July 1881, Sitting Bull and the remaining Hunk Papa left Canada, and surrendered to U.S. Military authorities at Fort Buford, Dakota Territory. After a brief period of imprisonment, Sitting Bull was released and settled in the Grand River region of modern day South Dakota. He later performed with Buffalo Bill Cody in his "Wild West Show," before being murdered by reservation police in 1890.

The reader may be interested in knowing that in 1877, the year after The Battle of Little Big Horn, another group of American Indians made a "run for the Canadian border." The Nez Perce Indian tribe, who were settled in Northeastern Oregon, were ordered to move to a reservation in Idaho. The Nez Perce, led by Chief Joseph, rejected that order and decided to settle in Canada. Chief Joseph had studied U.S. Army tactics and knew his people would be pursued. He led the Nez Perce on a journey of 1,300 miles across Oregon, Washington, Idaho, Wyoming and finally Montana, pursued the entire time by General Oliver Howard and a force of over 800 soldiers. General Howard was amazed at how Chief Joseph used U.S. Army tactics such as advance and rear guards, skirmish lines, and field fortifications to frustrate the pursing soldiers. On several occasions,

Nez Perce warriors defeated General Howard's forces in open combat.

Chief Joseph was not, however, a "miracle worker." In early October 1877 an army column commanded by General Nelson Miles moved into position to block the Nez Perce advance to Canada. A bloody four-day battle ensued and finally on October 5th Chief Joseph surrendered – only 40 miles from the perceived sanctuary of the Canadian border.[10]

Crazy Horse surrendered to the army in May 1877 and was bayoneted to death by a soldier in Fort Robinson, Nebraska, later that year. One of the greatest American leaders in history was dead.

Ironically enough, the final major battle on the western frontier also involved the 7th Cavalry and the Sioux. On December 29, 1890, two weeks after Sitting Bull was murdered, the 7th massacred over 150 Sioux men, women, and children at Wounded Knee, South Dakota.[11] This was the final "act" in a long and bloody period of years on the western frontier.

There are probably few, if any, battles that have provoked and prompted more questions than Little Big Horn. Why didn't Custer wait for Terry and Gibbon? Why did Reno not press home his attack on the village? Why did Benteen not respond to Custer's orders to join him? As for those soldiers dug in at the Reno/Benteen position, why did they not follow army doctrine and proceed to the sound of the firing when it was clear that Custer and his men were heavily

---

[10] It is doubtful he would have been welcomed by Canadian authorities. The Canadian government would likely have simply ignored the Nez Perce as they did with Sitting Bull's Hunk Papa, in the hope they'd return to the United States.

[11] For an excellent and moving account of this incident readers are encouraged to read Dee Brown's "Bury My Heart At Wounded Knee."

engaged in battle? And what would have happened to Custer and his men if Reno and Benteen had done the above?

There are no clear answers to those questions. To be fair to Custer, it is the opinion of the author and many others that most if not all other army officers would have made the same decision as Custer did. That is to attack after he received word of the Indian children discovering the dropped supplies. He had no way of knowing those children were not part of the main village, and history had shown that Indian villages always, without exception, "broke camp" and scattered when there was news of soldiers nearby. Custer could not know that the mood in this village was very different. (If General Crook had sent news about the Rosebud battle at least Custer would have had "an inkling" that this village might in fact stand and fight him.) It must also be pointed out that General Terry and Colonel Gibbon arrived at the scene on June 27th – a full day late. Even if Custer had waited to the 26th, as originally envisioned by Terry, he would have been alone in his attack.

Many feel that if Major Reno had pushed on with his initial attack that his entire force would have been destroyed. There is probably some strong validity to that opinion.

Others feel that there was no way Benteen and his three companies could have fought their way to Custer, and even if they did all they would have done was to have died with Custer and his 225 men. That may be true but it does not discount that fact that Benteen made no effort to obey Custer's orders. It also doesn't discount the fact that Reno and Benteen made no effort at all to move to Custer's aid when it was clear he was heavily engaged in battle. Is it possible that, if they had made even a strong feint towards Custer from their position, that may have drawn some of the Indians away from Custer, possibly allowing some of his men to escape? It certainly isn't far-fetched to think that was a possibility.

Custer deserves one piece of criticism in so far as the conduct of this battle is concerned. Worried about the village escaping him, he divided his regiment into three separate units (four if you count the pack train guarded by Company B) and deployed them in such a manner as to make it difficult for each to support the other. He also left Captain Benteen and Major Reno without a clear idea of what he was planning to do with his five companies. The end result was mass confusion amongst the officers of the Benteen and Reno battalions. It does stand to reason that if Benteen and Reno were aware of Custer's plan to strike the village from the rear, that they might have felt a greater impetus to attempt to reach him during the battle.

It may be surprising to the reader to discover that there is still an outstanding issue today in which George Armstrong Custer played a major role. In June 1980 the United States Supreme Court ruled that Congress had acted illegally in seizing the Black Hills back in 1875 and awarded the Sioux $15.5 million for the market value of the Black Hills in 1875 plus interest dating back to 1875. The interest added up to an additional $105 million. The Sioux to this date have refused the money, insisting they want their land back. There appears to be no settlement in sight for this issue.

Custer and the Sioux/Cheyenne have been perceived differently by history through the years. Shortly after the battle, Custer was portrayed as the brave "Boy General" killed with his gallant men in a despicable massacre by bloodthirsty savages. This view held well into the 20th century. By the 1960's, however, Custer and the Indians were seen in a vastly different light. Custer was now portrayed almost as a 19th century "Nazi" leading an army of barbarians into the west to steal land from the noble inhabitants.

There may be a grain of truth in both schools of thought. What can be said clearly here though is this. Both the soldiers of the 7th Cavalry and the warriors of the Sioux and Cheyenne nations were products of their time, and need to be judged by the standards of those times, not those of today. They were brave Americans fighting for their land and for their way of life. They need to be judged and honored in that light.

ABOUT THE AUTHOR

Craig Wallace was born and raised in Toronto, Ontario. He graduated from the University of Western Ontario in 1987 with a degree in history. He is the author of "A Slip in the Rain, the True Story of the 1967-72 Toronto Argonauts and the Fumble that Killed Canada's Team", and "The Forgotten Summit, A Canadian Perspective on the 1974 Canada Soviet Hockey Series. He currently lives in Hamilton, Ontario.

Made in the USA
Charleston, SC
10 March 2016